TIBURÓN

Edward A. Holsclaw II

FAITHFUL LIFE PUBLISHERS

NORTH FORT MYERS, FL

TIBURÓN

Second Edition
Paperback ISBN: 978-1-63073-399-5
Hard Cover ISBN: 978-1-63073-401-5
eBook: 978-1-63073-400-8

Published and printed by:
Faithful Life Publishers • North Fort Myers, FL 33903
888.720.0950 • info@FaithfulLifePublishers.com
www.FaithfulLifePublishers.com

Published in the United States of America
25 24 23 22 21   1 2 3 4 5

For

Dad, Mom, and Grandslam

Thanks for always being there…
and believing in me.

CHAPTER ONE

The sea was a dark, rolling cloud filled with majestic hues of emerald and cobalt. Faint trails of illumination from the night's full moon danced lightly atop the waves, like fireflies kissing the midnight. The light surgically penetrated the water's darkness, casting golden glimpses into the murky depths below. Through the quiet stillness, a pod of killer whales moved effortlessly through the layers of aquatic motion with respected ease, occasionally penetrating the timeless barrier forever separating the two distinct worlds for the necessary and much welcomed breath of air.

Foooossshhhh!

The huffs of the killer whales as they surfaced, mixed with the tranquility of water bursts and falling droplets demonstrated a regal dominance over their world. There was no creature more revered in these waters. Normally they cut fearlessly through the underworld as a powerful group, however, something was amiss tonight, causing the great whales to swim out of sync. Instinctively, they moved with guarded caution, sensing the uneasiness in their world.

Without warning, a chilling and fateful cry of terror escaped from the group's smallest member. A vulnerable calf's muffled cry was too late to serve any other purpose than the announcement of impending doom. Unable to react to the silent and seemingly unseen attack, the herd was left unprotected and unable to defend themselves from their assassins. Echolocation, the normally super-efficient method of communication and hunting was rendered useless in the swarm of chaotic fury. In the midst of this confusion, the water, littered with torn pieces of flesh, became a pitiable blur of thick dark liquid as blood exploded beneath the otherwise calm surface.

The attack, mercifully swift and reckless, seemed to be a feasting territorial claim of dominance, but for the executioner, it had been instinctually—pleasurable.

CHAPTER TWO

Bill Cramer was stiff, sore, and more than a little worn out from the flu he had suffered through the week before. He almost wished he had stayed home this time. They had been sitting on his favorite boat out in the middle of the serene darkness for what seemed liked days, instead of just hours. The slow rocking of the boat did little to aid his still queasy stomach as he choked back the bile that suddenly began to rise in his burning throat.

"Nature sure has a funny way of letting you know you're not a kid anymore," Bill groaned as he ineffectively rubbed his throbbing head. Nothing—not even a nibble. He should not have come. The stupid overgrown fish were probably all asleep, which was exactly where he should be, he thought angrily, wincing as he slowly stood for a much-needed stretch.

"Pops, pass me another bottle of water. This here shark fishin' stirs up a powerful thirst," Bill managed to say, trying to hold his eyes open.

George Litton had gone by the name Pops for as long as Bill could remember. It suited him. He had a sun dried, leathery face with unusually large wrinkles produced from years of overexposure to the Florida sun. He also moaned and complained more than most men twice his age.

"Here, catch. We wouldn't want such a sissy to deteriorate," Pops chuckled maliciously.

"I think you mean dehydrate, you dummy," Hank laughed, shaking his head.

"Whatever, ya little slug. Next time you buy the water!" Pops said sarcastically as he sat back and scanned the peaceful water. "Wonder what's got the sharks spooked tonight?" he spoke again, trying to change the subject. He had gotten into the same argument several times before with Hank over his poor choice of words and his patience was running dangerously thin this night. "We've been out here all night and we aren't even gettin' any nibblin'. I always thought shark fishing was best at night."

"Don't worry, Pops. It's only 'bout 3:00 a.m. We still got a good two or three more hours till dawn. Besides, it could be a whole lot worse; you could be home in bed listenin' to your ol' lady snore." Hank tauntingly laughed. Bill chuckled to himself as he threw another bucket of chum into the water. Watching Hank goad Pops into a fury was every bit as fun as catching monster sharks could be.

Bill considered himself lucky. He had done well for himself as a fisherman down here. Key West had earned a reputation for poor availability and even poorer markets ever since the boom in the 60s. Still, he had managed to carve himself out a nice little niche and live comfortably, while expanding his fleet to include four other boats.

The three of them had been doing this Tuesday night run for sharks for almost a decade. They had a running bet as to who could catch the biggest, the nastiest, the most, or just about any other adjective you could come up with to keep the sport interesting.

Bill knew that some nights you had it, and others you just did not. Tonight, unfortunately, looked like the latter. But he had fun just the same. Pops was always complaining, and Hank was always pulling stupid pranks or inciting Pops to riot, leaving himself, as usual, to mediate and keep the peace.

"Are y'all about ready to go back? I don't think we're gonna have any luck," Pops urged as he stared blankly at the tip of his rod.

"Well, I guess I'm ready," sighed Bill. Anxious to get home and sleep off the aftereffects of his recent illness, he turned to Hank and asked, "What about you? Hank? Hank! Wake up you ol' fart."

"I'm awake. I was just resting my eyes," Hank grumbled, wiping at the drool that had started to gather at the corner of his mouth and slowly roll down his chin.

"Yea right! And I'm Jacques Cousteau and this here's the Calypso. Are you ready to go?" Pops asked impatiently.

"Yea, I guess so. Y'all er' never gonna beat my records anyway," Hank proudly pointed out.

Bill laughed to himself, realizing Hank had a point. "All right, let's bring the lines in, boys."

"My pleasure," Hank obliged, reaching out for his rod just as it suddenly bent down sharply with terrible force. The sound of the line flying from the reel made a loud, and familiar, screeching sound.

"Yee-ha, I got me one!" Hank proclaimed with joy, leaping up and seizing the frantically jumping rod. He held onto it tightly as Bill hurriedly helped him to buckle into the chair, securely hooking the rod to his belt. Hank took off the drag and tried to reel it in a little, only to realize whatever had the end of his line was definitely out of his league.

"This ain't no minnow we got here, boys! It's a real monster. I can't even reel it in!" Hank screamed through clenched teeth, the muscles in his arms already trembling as he strained against the unseen pressure.

Bill and Pops frantically rushed toward Hank in an effort to assist their friend, barely noticing their own poles scattering across the floor of the boat as they were yanked, one after the other, into the water.

"What is this thing?" Pops screamed.

Bill had never experienced anything like this before. His boat was under attack by an unknown entity concealed in the murky depths. He struggled clumsily to stay on his feet as he felt a startling hammering over and over against the groaning hull. The breaking and splintering planks underneath were being ripped away with ease. The gnawing sound was almost deafening to Bill's ears. It was as if the water itself was alive and devouring his boat.

"Unhook me! I can't hold this devil fish much longer!" Hank bellowed amidst the chaos. His screams brought Bill back to reality, and he and Pops tried desperately to unhook the belt from around Hank's waist. As the fishing line reached its end, Hank was stripped abruptly from his chair and dragged across the deck like a rag doll. When he reached the edge of the boat, he braced his feet against the railing to counteract the tremendous force taunting him at the other end of the line.

Unexpectedly, the line slacked and Hank was able to loosen his grip. His eyes remained transfixed on the point where the line disappeared into the swirling darkness below. Never taking his eyes from the water, his hand fumbled blindly for the buckle that tethered him to the monster. Before he could free himself of the harness, the line became taut again with such force it ripped Hank right over the side of the boat and into the water. It happened so fast that neither Bill nor Pops was able to make any attempt to save him.

Hank's screams were immediately swallowed by the sounds of a splash and the merciless slaughter that ensued. He was dead before he could taste the salt rushing in over his tongue and gushing down his throat as he opened his mouth to scream.

By the time the others reached the place of Hank's violent removal, they could barely make out the large dark stain on the surface below. The awful sounds of the attack on the boat ceased, only to be replaced by the quiet calm of the ocean. All was eerily still and silent.

"Hank!" Bill yelled. "Hank!"

"Oh, sweet mother of Mary! What just happened? I can't... I just—I just can't..." Pops screamed teary eyed. "Somebody tell me just what that is out there! I did not sign on for this, man," he whined.

"Hit the spotlight and quiet down!" Bill roared, standing motionless at the side of the boat, staring in shock into the depths where he had last seen his friend. He was terrified, but the thought of becoming the next meal pushed his body to respond by reflex. He reached up on his tiptoes to unhook the light and slowly scanned the area where Hank was pulled overboard.

"Hank! Hank!" Pops joined in the chant.

It was useless. There was no answer. The water remained silent, dark, and ominous. As usual, the sea told no secrets.

"Pops, keep looking. I'm going down below to radio the authorit..."

The boat jerked to the left, knocking Bill forcefully off his feet. The unseen terror returned and the boat was under attack again. Bill hurried down the stairs as he tried to counterbalance himself against the onslaught, but instead he bumped against the railing and wall with every hit from the outside forces. He managed to reach the radio just as the cabin went pitch dark. The power was gone. Everything shut down in an instant.

"Why now? You couldn't give me one more minute?" Bill lashed out in the darkness. Feeling helpless and alone, he winced as the sweat dripped into his eyes, making them burn.

"Bill? What happened? Did you cut the power?" Pops yelled from above.

Ignoring Pops' question, Bill concentrated on locating the problem. He hastily fumbled his way through the darkened room toward the back-up generator.

"Oh, man! Not now!" Bill muttered as water, now flooding the cabin floor, swallowed his foot. His mind swam frantically in circles searching for a way out of this predicament. *What do I do now,* he distractedly asked himself.

The incessant pounding grew louder and louder. Bill's ears began to ache under the relentless attack. The tossing movement of the boat had begun to taper off, yet the water flowed in more rapidly. Abandoning hope, Bill stood terrified, unable to calculate his next move. He hastily tried to back away from the influx of rising water, but could find no dry wood. Whatever was out there was going to find a way in, and Bill knew he could do little to stop it.

CHAPTER THREE

The challenge they had just faced was a formidable one, but to dominate and conquer was their sole purpose for existence. Their victim had yielded sparse amounts of palatable food compared to the size of its body. The harsh exterior could not be digested, but the food that dwelled within was something new to them and very much worth the effort. It was alien, unlike anything they had ever tasted before and they desperately hungered for more.

This night, their first night in a new world, food was plentiful. They utterly mutilated and devoured everything in their path. They were an indomitable swarm the likes of which this world's waters had never seen. There was no opponent worthy of their challenge, for they worked as a well-trained team—the only mercy given was that of a quick death. All that were unfortunate enough to cross their path was extinguished ferociously.

Darkness gradually disappeared bathed in a faint glow from the outside world as night gave birth to dawn. They had never experienced this strange luminescence, but paid little attention to the transformation for they were the ultimate predators, an extraordinarily fast adaptation mechanism made them so. They sensed that prey was close and an overwhelming, instinctual desire for blood consumed them. With a single mindedness, the horde set out on their next conquest with only one purpose—to kill.

CHAPTER FOUR

Jeffrey Brigham laid the *Florida Herald* on the kitchen counter and looked contentedly out his window. Turtle Beach in Key West had become his home after retirement. He had come to know well that which welcomed his view from almost every window of his home as Old Blue. In the six years he had lived there, he had only known a few rare occasions when Old Blue was not as blue as the skyline that it married on the horizon.

Turtle Beach's small town atmosphere, scattered with quaint little homes, vacation resorts, and condos was what drew Jeffrey here years ago. It was Florida's best-kept secret for the simple fact that it was not yet commercialized much. There was only one golf course, and no water slides or amusement parks to speak of. In fact, except for the second week of July when the town hosted the Turtle Beach International Pro-Spearfishing Tournament, the place was pretty dull. Jeffrey liked it that way. He dreaded the crowds that would pour in today like he dreaded a rash he could not reach to scratch. This year, he decided he would stay at his beach house at all costs, only venturing out in extreme emergencies.

Jeffrey gulped down the last swig of grapefruit juice and set his glass in the sink. *Ah, this is great*, Jeffrey thought, standing in the open sliding glass door. The sun's rays blanketed him with a warm sensation his soul felt nowhere else on earth. The sticky ocean breeze carried the faint, familiar smells of sea life he had grown to appreciate. As he went about his morning ritual of stretching his tired, but toned body, he glanced over to the ever-so-inviting Olympic sized pool where he would swim laps after returning from his daily four mile run up and down the beach.

Jeffrey jogged over to the path and made his way cautiously down the hill towards the beach. The constant movement of wind from the ocean was always an ally, fooling his body into believing his workouts did not cause him to sweat much. While still on the path, something happened to catch Jeffrey's eye in the distance. He squinted against the glare of the sun, wondering what it was he saw. About a half mile down the beach, something big had washed ashore.

Picking up his usual pace from a jog to a sprint, he hit the beach running along the water's edge. As he grew closer to the massive objects, intrigued by the mystery of his find, his heartbeat raced fiercely. Moments later though, as he better perceived the sheer magnitude of the objects that lay scattered along the beach a wave of caution twisted in his gut. Jeffrey slowed his pace a bit, unsure of what he was facing.

He had seen his share of the usual beach sightings: jellyfish, turtles, fish, and loads of trash. If you could name it, he had seen it washed ashore—but nothing like this.

"There weren't any storms or unusually high tides last night. What could have beached something of this size?" Jeffrey muttered to himself, perplexed as he drew closer. "What is this?"

He slowed to a swaggering saunter, his hands propped on his hips. He unfortunately had the answer now, and he did not want to get any closer.

Walking in slow motion, he looked at the scene in horror. Swallowing hard to keep his breakfast down, Jeffrey pulled his t-shirt up over his nose and mouth to guard against the stench of rotting flesh that surrounded the air around him. Finally, overcome by the sight and smell of the horrific scene, Jeffrey quickly dropped to his knees and lost the battle with his stomach. He did everything he could to hold it in, but his breakfast and that awful tasting grapefruit juice violently exploded from his mouth and shot onto the beach.

What he saw was horrific! Pieces and chunks of killer whales were scattered all down the shoreline. Jeffrey searched his mind for rational explanations. *What could have happened to them? Who or what could have slaughtered these magnificent creatures?*

He could tell they were killer whales only by the coloring of the skin, for everything else had been brutally mangled to unrecognizable proportions. Jeffrey carefully walked around the bloody pieces, desperately scanning the area for answers, or at least clues. It was then he saw something that brought tears flooding his eyes. A baby killer whale's severed head, in perfect condition, ominously bobbed up and down in the water; the eyes appeared to be pleading for help, but that help was all too gone.

Jeffrey turned and dashed back to the house to use his telephone. He knew something was terribly wrong and he needed to tell someone quickly.

The race back to his house seemed to take forever. His mind reeled with the vivid pictures, now forever etched in his memory. He reached the back door and slung it open, hastily grabbing for the ancient telephone anchored to the wall. Clumsily dropping it, Jeffrey barely caught it by the cord before he wrestled it to his ear. His panting was uncontrollable and his heart pounded, causing his fingers to fumble over the dial and press the wrong numbers.

"Get a hold of yourself!" he shouted as he slammed the receiver against the countertop. Taking a deep breath, he carefully started over—9-1-1. The rapping of his heart echoed hollowly against the earpiece as he trembled nervously in anticipation.

A calm voice answered after the second ring, "911, what is your emergency?"

CHAPTER FIVE

"This looks like a nice spot. Drop the anchor, mate!" Nic theatrically stated in a fake Australian accent. "Let's get a little wet!"

"Sure Cap'n, there she goes," answered Ben, throwing the anchor from the two-man catamaran and drenching Nic and his California bleach blonde hair.

Nic Petse was an Adonis. At six foot-two and 190 pounds, his statuesque figure and chiseled jaw line, combined with his sparkling white smile and pale blue eyes, made him just about any woman's dream.

"Just wait till we go below; I owe ya!" Nic smiled mischievously.

The two young men were there to scope out a good location to spearfish. The 8th Annual Turtle Beach Pro-Spearfishing Tournament was just one day away, and Nic and Ben were the likely favorites. They had been friends and teammates for the last five years. They met at the University of California where Ben Holse had received a Bachelor's degree in Communications before deciding to pursue a career in professional spearfishing because the money was good and he loved it.

Ben was, for the most part, the serious conservative side of the team. With his dark bushy hair, chubby round face, and unkempt goatee, he was an uncharacteristic looking companion for Nic, but the two worked well together and had formed a very tight bond over the years.

Wild man Nic, on the other hand, finally dropped out of college after attending three schools in five years. School was just not in his blood and he knew it. He was more interested in having a good time than in biology. Why should he waste his time in school when he loved to spearfish and he was making good money at it? He was always looking for the next adventure and loved to party.

Ben spit into his mask and smeared it over the lens as he scanned the surrounding water. "Are you ready, guy?"

"I was born ready, Bubba," Nic excitedly answered. "Let's kick some fishy tail today!"

Nic sprang from the small catamaran and did a not-so-Olympian flip into the water causing a huge splash.

"You're crazy! You know that?" Ben laughed. The boat dipped up and down causing him to almost lose his balance.

Nic surfaced and shouted, "Hey, throw me my snorkel and spear gun. Let's go, man!"

"Alright, Dork-nose! How's the water anyway?" Ben knew he should not have bothered asking; Nic was never serious.

"It's as warm and toasty as one of your mama's hugs!" Nic said smiling.

Ben frowned, knowing full well what a lady's man old love-'em-and-leave-'em Nic could be. "I'll thank you to leave my mama out of any scenario going through the cesspool in your head."

Nic grinned apologetically as he stared childishly up at Ben. "Okay, I can't wait any longer. I'm heading on down."

"Happy hunting! I'll be down in a second."

Ben had trouble putting on his second flipper, but with some agonizing skin pulling maneuvers and a few grunts, he eventually got the thing on. He loved the exhilaration right before entering the water. Everything seemed so calm and quiet and right with the world. He sighed; this was his own personal heaven.

Ben surveyed the area as far as he could see. It was his precautionary ritual, for he did not want to take any life threatening chances. He noticed a flock of seagulls skimming the water's surface in the distance and turned to look behind him. Everything looked safe as Ben peered down into the water below, but something caught his eye as he glanced back up again. Far off in the distance, he could see there was something unnatural occurring, although he could not quite make it out. A dark mass slowly moved in his direction.

Splassshhhh!

Ben turned, startled, only to see the tips of Nic's flippers disappear into the deep blue. Surfacing for air about 75 yards out, Nic quickly dove back under.

"Nic!" screamed Ben. It was no use. There was no way Nic would hear him now. Ben spun around in a circle, trying to locate the uninvited guests. "Oh no!"

Illogically closer than they had been just a few seconds before, the normally bright blue ocean had turned to awful ebony. Dorsal fins protruded grotesquely from the water in overwhelming numbers and their speed was incomprehensible. Ben had never seen anything swim as fast as these creatures.

"C'mon. C'mon—come up for air," Ben hopelessly begged, praying they were just dolphins coming to play. Unfortunately, it was not to be and he knew what that meant.

"Sharks! Sharks!"

Ben frantically searched the water where Nic had last submerged, but there was no sign of his partner. "Nic! Nic!" he cried madly.

The sharks advanced on them at an unearthly pace.

"Lord, give me a miracle!" Ben pleaded while he beat the water with an oar hoping to get Nic's attention.

Nic broke the water's surface for a quick breath. "Nic!" Ben screamed, but unfortunately he was even farther away this time and was facing the opposite direction. Nic had no sooner popped up to catch his breath and he was back down again.

"Nic!" Ben shouted in desperation. He turned to see if maybe the intruders had headed in another direction, but that was only wishful thinking. They were almost on top of him, in a few more seconds he would be enveloped by the ungodly creatures.

Ben believed his mind had to be playing tricks on him. There seemed to be hundreds of dorsal fins moving at speeds that defied all rational laws of nature. Their black fins were jagged, coming to a sharp point on top, and they cut through the water in a razor-like fashion. As they drew ever closer, the realization shook the very foundation of Ben's reality. These were not your typical sharks.

Ben's mind raced, *What can I do?* A whirlwind of useless options flew through his mind for what seemed an eternity, but was in reality only seconds. He reached over and pulled the anchor up, hand over fist, as fast as he could. His breathing became sporadic and all he could hear was his heart pounding in his ears. With every tug, he gasped for air as the threat to his own existence was hideously confirmed.

Boom, boom, boom! The catamaran was under fire by the vile creatures. Ben dropped the anchor and it plummeted into the murky depths. All he could do was hang on as they relentlessly hammered the small boat.

Nic was having the time of his life. He had already snagged a few big ones, and was ready to come up for some oxygen. *Could you be any slower, Ben,* he thought belligerently.

Nic turned in the direction of the boat and began to ascend to the surface, both for air and to see what was keeping his buddy. He shook his head, trying to clear his vision, as the light overhead suddenly disappeared, leaving him nearly blind in the dark sea. *Did a cloud cover the sun?* No, he reasoned, it was too dark for that. His eyes again tested the waters above. "What the heck!" Nic expelled the rest of his air supply as water engorged his lungs. The sight before him was a dark ugly blanket, alive with terror. The water was full of sharks, but these were not normal sharks, they were grisly. Nic frantically searched for the safety of the boat, but it too late. The creatures converged on him like black metal shavings to a powerful magnet before he had any time to react.

His life would soon be over, so he did what anyone else would have done and put up the fight of his life. Praying for a moment of mercy, Nic aimed his spear gun into the mass and shot—futilely— only braising a pectoral fin as they sped toward him for the kill. He drew back to hit the first one, but the gun slipped from his hand. Swinging his fists and kicking his feet furiously, he tried to scare them so he could work his way to the surface. Alas, there were too many of them.

Wave after wave, they continued to come as he fought for his life. He struck a couple of them, only scraping the skin from his now bloodied fists, but his efforts had little affect on the masses. They violently swarmed upon him. Nic could feel each bite penetrating his thin skin. The beasts lunged into him with dagger sharp teeth and surgical accuracy. A chunk of his side was ripped away, and then his leg. He was being torn apart from all directions. The last thing he remembered was darkness as jaws enclosed over his face and the flesh was pulled from his skull.

There was no pain, just rapid coolness. It was over in a matter of seconds, and he would have wanted it that way. The creatures consumed Nic with piranha-like definitiveness until all that remained was a thick pool of crimson slowly dissipating into the vastness of the sea.

Ben knew Nic was gone. He had not been able to take his eyes from the feeding frenzy below, and now the bloodstained waters vomited from the depths completely surrounded him. His boat was still under attack, and since Nic was gone more sharks joined forces against him. He held on for all he was worth, even though he knew the boat would not hold up much longer. If he was lucky, death would come swiftly.

Like most who are about to die violently and unexpectedly, Ben pleaded for deliverance where there was none. "Help! Somebody, please help me!" Unfortunately, Ben's frightened shrieks went unheard. The pitch-black creatures were everywhere. Their heads surfaced above the water as if to sneer with hypnotic cold black eyes, penetrating Ben's very soul. Others systematically rammed and pounded the boat. Their jaws, full of awful rows of jagged sharp teeth, yearned for the vital fluid of life.

Ben knew he was losing the battle, for the small boat was sinking fast. "Leave me alone!" he pleaded, but the frenzy only continued. He struggled to his feet and clumsily climbed the sail to buy a few more moments of precious life. Ben slipped, catching himself just over the edge of the boat. He instantly scrambled to pull himself up out of harm's way, but something seized the side of his head and throat, whipping him from the boat. The stabbing pain was tremendous and his dying cries for help were quickly silenced as he was violently pulled below to a horrific bone-grinding death.

CHAPTER SIX

"Good morning, Dr. Wyatt! How are ya doing?" Jeffrey Brigham spoke anxiously.

"Pretty good. How about yourself?" Dr. Kurt Wyatt asked, puzzled.

"As well as can be expected after what I just saw this morning, I suppose," he paused briefly to catch his breath. "This is Jeffrey Brigham. I'm sorry to call you at home. The university gave me your number. I hope you don't mind."

"That's alright. What can I do for you Mr. Brigham?"

"Well... it's something I think you might be interested in."

"Yes, go on, Mr. Brigham," Dr. Wyatt prodded him.

"Well, I live in Turtle Beach, and this morning I went for my usual jog along the water and you wouldn't believe what I discovered."

"What did you find?" Dr. Wyatt asked patiently.

"Well, I called the police and they came over and said it was nothing. They just blew it off! I'm sure there's more to it though; it doesn't take a rocket scientist to know that it just doesn't seem right."

"What is it?" Dr. Wyatt asked politely, growing impatient.

"Doctor, there must have been a dozen killer whales slaughtered all over the beach. It was awful. And when I say slaughtered, I mean s-l-a-u-g-h-t-e-r-e-d, slaughtered!"

"Can you speculate how it happened? Is there any type of evidence?" Dr. Wyatt asked, his curiosity aroused.

"I really can't even begin to guess what did this. It looks like a busload of lumberjacks took chainsaws to them! I just couldn't believe it, so I decided to call someone at Florida University about it."

"I'm glad you called. I've never heard of anything like this before in my life. I'm as good as there!"

"Doctor, the police are sending a city crew over to clean up, so you'd better hurry."

"Can you ask them not to touch anything till I get there? I'll call the police department on my end and do the same," Dr. Wyatt ordered. "I'll be there in roughly two and a half hours."

Dr. Wyatt hurriedly took down all the necessary information and directions and stopped by the university to pick up his equipment and supplies. He hoped it was not just another goose chase, but in this business you chased the goose quite often, hoping one would have a golden egg. He was very curious as to what could have caused such damage to the top predator in the ocean. Either Mr. Brigham was severely exaggerating the situation or something had to be terribly wrong, for only man could have performed such an evil task. What else could cause such destruction?

Dr. Kurt Wyatt, a world-renowned marine biologist with so many letters after his name you could play a good game of scrabble, had worked for the Florida University Oceanography Department for twelve years, specializing in shark research. In all his years as student, teacher, scientist, and researcher he had never heard of such a thing. He knew he had to get to the bottom of it, and fast. Sensing he was riding the crest of one of the biggest oceanographic discoveries of all time, Dr. Wyatt picked up his cellular phone from the passenger seat of his Jeep Cherokee and dialed the number for information as he sped towards Turtle Beach.

"The number for the Turtle Beach Police Department, please," Dr. Wyatt politely asked the operator.

CHAPTER SEVEN

The harsh Florida sun basted the shoreline. *Thank God for the breeze*, Dr. Wyatt thought as he and Jeffrey Brigham arrived at the site of the mutilated whales. The local police department had covered the location with several giant blue tarps in an attempt to curb public curiosity. Chief Robert Cutlit had been cooperative over the phone, and said he would leave the site *as is* so Dr. Wyatt could investigate with as little human intervention as possible. The chief, however, insisted the whole affair was nothing to be alarmed over. Contrary to his statement, the look on his face suggested he actually believed differently.

"Well, here it is Dr. Wyatt," Jeffrey said in a squeamish voice. The stench was thick and unbearable as Dr. Wyatt set down his equipment cases and took out a couple of surgical masks and a pair of gloves.

"Here you go. I think you will need this?" Dr. Wyatt grimaced, holding his breath as he tossed a mask to Jeffrey.

"Thanks," Jeffrey said appreciatively.

Dr. Wyatt loved being out in the field. This was why he chose this profession to begin with and he simply could not get enough of it. How a person could spend their entire life shackled behind a desk, confined by four walls and the occasional window was beyond his understanding. He was thirty-nine years old, still a young age compared to his peers at the university, and he felt both physically and mentally like a teenager. He thought it was probably due to the fact that he loved what he did. He had a passion for the ocean and everything it housed. It was not like work to him. It was his passion, and his life simply revolved around it.

He had been married for six years, although now widowed; his wife had died in a tragic car accident. Ever since that horrible day two years ago, he had gradually grown used to being alone, never finding interest in anyone that even came close to his Miranda.

"Let's see what we have here," Dr. Wyatt announced as he glanced up to find Jeffrey squinting in preparation for the nightmare he was about to look upon again.

Dr. Wyatt quickly jerked the tarp off, not expecting to see such horror underneath. His brain instantly seized and he could not believe what his eyes were telling him. Words left him as he mumbled unintelligible phrases.

Holy Moses! Dr. Wyatt quickly remembered his promise to the chief. For that matter, the university did not want him to discuss any of his findings with the public either, which meant he would have to tone down his emotions a bit with Jeffrey nearby.

"What do ya think, Doc? What did this?"

Dr. Wyatt didn't answer, he was still shocked and perplexed at the unnatural destruction before him. The truth was he did not really know what cause this. He had never seen anything like it before. It appeared that as many as a dozen Orcas had been fiercely massacred. The opposition had to be tremendous in size or numbers to kill the likes of one killer whale, not to mention an entire pod.

The teeth marks and bite radiuses vaguely resembled that of sharks, but the bite patterns were different. This was not a typical frenzied shark attack. There was too much control, precision, and purpose to the wounds inflicted on these animals. There was no way this could have been done by sharks. It did not make any sense. All of his years of study and experience gave him no explanations. His earlier assumptions had proven correct; he knew he was onto something major. His emotions ran the gauntlet through sadness, excitement, and fear of the unknown.

"Well Doctor, what do you make of this?" Jeffrey's tone was vaguely demanding.

Dr. Wyatt was pulled back to reality by the harsh tone of Jeffrey's voice. "I cannot be certain. I will need much more time to study this." He scurried over to his bags and pulled out a cellular phone. "I need to make a few calls. Please excuse me."

He had to get the whales into refrigeration quickly. They were already beginning to decay and every second stole precious evidence. His first call was to his assistant, Shane Briggs, who would bring the Mobile Oceanography Laboratory (MOL), a high-tech oceanography laboratory on wheels that resembled an RV. The specimens could then be kept fresh and could be studied on location. His second call was to Chief Cutlit to inform him of his plans. The chief was not very interested, but he was happy someone else would be cleaning up the mess.

Dr. Wyatt stared at the whales for a moment before his gaze shifted out to sea. There was sadness in his heart. *What on God's earth could have done such a savage thing?* And yet, even as he stared thoughtfully toward the horizon, they were moving ever closer to their next victim—relentlessly hunting.

CHAPTER EIGHT

Keen senses picked up the vibrations and buzzing roars zigzagging directly in front of them. The noise and the electromagnetic pulses of the prey grew louder as they strategically positioned themselves for the kill. Each knew of the others' places in the attack formation as they surrounded the target area, making it impossible for anyone or anything to penetrate their walls of doom.

Ahead, two teenage boys cut through the waves on their jet skis, smacking the water's surface and soaring high into the moist air before splashing back down to the sea. Laughing and yelping, the boys feared for nothing, having no knowledge of the terror lurking below.

The sharks quickly closed in for the kill, but this prey was different, the speed and patterns at which these loud beings traveled made them a worthy opponent, a challenge they welcomed. Increasing their speed to a mind-numbing pace, they bounded for the surface. An instinctual thirst for blood drove them as they converged upon their target.

The younger of the two boys had just hit a wave and was airborne about five feet from the surface. Looking down for his landing, he noticed the pale blue water that should have been there to welcome him had turned to a cold dismal black. In the split-second it had taken to hit the water, he submerged partially; it was then they made their move.

The blackness was alive with terror. A blur of fins, razor sharp teeth, and sea foam flashed before the boy's eyes. All of his jet ski experience left him as he lost his balance and tumbled helplessly, end over end, into the perilous sea. The boy reached for the safety of the surface, but the killers closed in upon him with swift, militant accuracy and the water erupted with violence. The boy only saw a glimpse of his killers before his body was ripped apart from all directions and consumed entirely by the merciless beasts. They showed no compassion, for they yearned for the kill and the taste of blood.

Unaware of his brother's terrible fate, the other boy saw his brother's jet ski bobbing quietly in the water fifty yards away. Immediately turning his ski around, he headed to locate his brother. Halfway to the abandoned jet ski, he noticed the crimson blackness of the water and the numerous fins that protruded, cutting in synchronized definitiveness, now moving towards him.

Should he try to find his brother or make a run for the shore? Every instinct told him to save himself. He knew it was probably too late to save his brother. Gunning the engine, he propelled himself and the jet ski towards the shoreline, but they still gained on him fast. Their speed was unnatural. Even knowing he was surrounded, he pushed forward in vain as they relentlessly battered the machine. Through the mist and the waves, he saw the terrifying figures— revoltingly hideous, to say the least. Their haunting eyes, cold and lifeless, shot straight through his soul as if he were looking into hell itself.

The impacts against his machine were too great and numerous for him to hold on much longer. There was only forty yards between life and death, but he doubted he would make it. Those doubts quickly became a surreal reality. Thirty yards from shore his jet ski was hit head on with terrible force and he was flung to his certain death.

Violently crashing into the water, he instinctually found his bearings and frantically swam for the beach. He felt massive thuds against his legs before a cool sensation flooded his body. He dared not look back, but swam like mad for the shoreline. His arms flailed as fast as he could, but his forward progress stalled abruptly and he sank below the surface.

No! Why am I sinking? his thoughts screamed, his brain failing to realize his limbs were no more. His life was ripped away as the feeding frenzy ensued until all was savagely consumed.

The ocean returned to its formerly peaceful state, swallowing the blood of its young victims. The hunt was over. The thrill of the chase was momentarily satisfied, but the thirst for blood still lingered. This all-consuming thirst was their simple purpose, their only reason for being.

CHAPTER NINE

"Dr. Wyatt, it's Dr. Paige," Shane announced, anxiously handing the phone over. Shane stood a stocky five feet, five inches, and his straight brown hair and hazel eyes revealed a boyish charm. His best selling point, however, was his effortless smile. Pearly white teeth lined his most noticeable attribute, and distinct dimples stood at either side like beacons of welcome. Concealed beneath his white lab coat was a bronzed athletic physique comfortably clothed in cut-off blue jean shorts and a white tank top. His worn out leather sandals only hinted at his beachcomber attitude towards life. He grew up on the beach and he would not have it any other way.

"Dr. Paige, thank you for returning my call so quickly. My name is Dr. Kurt Wyatt, head of Florida University's Oceanography Department." As confident as he sounded, Dr. Wyatt felt as though he was dreaming, for he was speaking to the leading shark expert in the world. All five of her books were stacked on his nightstand and he had practically memorized her studies. She was very well respected and a paragon of knowledge in her field.

"Hello, Dr. Wyatt. I don't stand on formality, so please call me Amanda."

"Sure, then please call me Kurt."

"Thank you, Kurt. I'm very familiar with your work. I've read several of your studies, especially on territorialism in sharks and

30

the systematic extinction of certain species by the fishing industry. They were quite enlightening. At any rate, how can I or the National Shark Institute be of assistance to you?"

Dr. Wyatt was momentarily taken aback by the fact that she already knew who he was. In his wildest dreams, he would not have expected to be on her radar.

"Well, I've discovered something here in the Florida Keys that is just unexplainable. I think, perhaps, something monumental has taken place here." Dr. Wyatt cleared his throat to calm his nerves. He knew he sounded a little too intense, but his emotions were taking over. He truly believed he was onto something of great significance to mankind.

"Please go on," Amanda urged.

"This is going to be hard for you to believe, but here goes." Dr. Wyatt painstakingly explained every detail, careful not to omit anything.

Dr. Paige hesitated momentarily to give herself some time for all the information to permeate her logic. "I've never heard of such an attack on killer whales."

There was brief silence.

"And the bite radiuses and patterns do not match any other documented species of shark or other aquatic life?"

"That's correct," Kurt quickly replied.

"I would very much like to take a look for myself, if you don't mind," she swelled with excitement at the notion of a new discovery.

"No, not at all. Actually, um… I was hoping you would." Kurt smiled and gave the thumbs up to Shane.

"That's great," Dr. Paige smiled ear to ear. "I'll be on the first available flight to the States."

"Alright! Let me give you the name and location of the..."

"No need. I'll have my secretary call you for the logistics and to give you my arrival time," Amanda cut in brusquely, her mind already filled with the variable possibilities of what lay ahead.

"That will be fine," said Kurt.

"Thank you for calling. I have so much to do to prepare. I'll see you later, Kurt."

"Thank you, and I look forward to working with you," Dr. Wyatt added, a tingling sensation spreading to every hair on his head. He was ecstatic to be working on what could develop into the most important find of this century, not to mention working with the world-renowned shark expert—Amanda Paige, the golden girl in her branch of oceanography. To be honest, he was also vaguely looking forward to seeing whether she was as pretty as she was in the pictures on the back of her books. It had been a long time since he'd noticed a woman, but as he and Shane went back to analyzing the specimens, he could not get Amanda's charming Australian accent out of his head.

CHAPTER TEN

Boom! Boom! Boom! The metal door on the MOL rattled violently, jolting Dr. Wyatt from his concentrated research and causing him to break the lead on his pencil.

"Every time…" he mumbled, rolling his eyes and tossing the fractured tip of the writing utensil into the trash can at his feet.

Expecting his guest and soon-to-be partner, Dr. Paige, to arrive soon, he rose from his chair to open the door, straining his eyes against the moonless night as he did. Flipping the wall switch up and down, he unsuccessfully tried to illuminate the area just outside the door, and only the startling movement of a shadow alerted him to someone's presence.

"Good evening, Doctor. Can I come inside?" a familiar deep voice asked, the shadow moving forward into the rectangle of light thrown onto the ground by the open doorway.

"Oh, Chief Cutlit, it's you!" the doctor exhaled, relief coloring every syllable. "Come on in. I was kind of expecting someone else. Is there something I can get you to drink?"

"I could sure go for some stiff coffee right about now."

Dr. Wyatt walked into the kitchen area and poured some coffee into two aquamarine ceramic mugs that prominently displayed the Florida University's logo. "How do you take yours?"

"Black; I don't drink it for the taste so that's the only way to have it."

"Chief, you're a man after my own heart," the doctor agreed, raising his mug in an unspoken toast. "Straight black, that's what keeps me going."

"So Doc, what have you come up with? Was it a rogue school of genetically altered piranhas, or the Loch Ness Monster?" the Chief chuckled, knowing he should be serious about this, but somehow still hoping there was an amusing, or at least boring, explanation of what he had seen on the beach. The uniformed chief was a lean wiry fellow who stood at six foot four and weighed about 190 pounds. He was in his mid-to-upper fifties, but gave the impression of a man much older. His aged and wrinkled face, full head of salt and pepper hair, and hunched over physique revealed to all his hardened life as a police officer.

"Well Chief, truthfully I've never in all of my experiences seen, or even heard of, this kind of an attack on killer whales. There's got to be some logical explanation for this," Kurt confided as he randomly shuffled through the paperwork on his desk. "The closest answer I can come up with, based on my findings so far, shows that it could be sharks. However, please understand the bite patterns and dimensions don't actually match up with any known species of shark. For that matter, I've never come across any living animal in the oceans that could take on one killer whale, much less twelve, and tear them beyond recognition like that."

"So, let me get this straight." The chief paused to take a swig of his java. "You don't know what did this?"

Kurt shrugged, "I'm still working on it. The world's leading expert on sharks should be walking through that door any minute to help figure this out. But my best guess at this point would be a school of chainsaws with fins."

The chief sighed as he set down his cup, "I think we might have more trouble than you think."

"What do you mean?" Dr. Wyatt automatically asked, his natural state of curiosity taking over.

"There have been two different missing persons reports filed within the last twenty-four hours. First, a prominent businessman from these parts and two of his buddies went shark fishing last night and they have yet to turn up. Also, two young boys who were out jet skiing this afternoon are also missing. I contacted the Coast Guard, but they haven't turned up anything yet. No bodies, no boats... nothing."

"Do you think these sharks, or whatever did that to the whales, could be responsible?" Chief Cutlit went on to inquire of Dr. Wyatt.

The possibility of these mysterious creatures attacking humans was branded in Dr. Wyatt's mind and this dose of reality hit him hard. "I hope not, but whatever created the carnage we saw on that beach… well," he paused and swallowed hard, "it's more than possible."

Both men stood silently, letting that possibility sink in for a moment.

"Okay," the police chief finally said, nodding his head in understanding. "Well, I don't mean to sound callous, but I'm going to grab something to eat. I have a sinking feeling time for mundane things, such as meals or showers, is gonna become mighty precious, if you get my meaning. If you come up with anything new, just give me a ring."

"I sure will."

"And Doc, I need those answers ASAP. Tomorrow at the crack of dawn the Turtle Beach International Pro-Spearfishing Tournament gets underway. We're talking about a lot of people out there in the water. If there's something dangerous out there, I need to know right away."

"I get it. I know how urgent this is. I'll talk to you soon. Thanks for stopping by, Chief."

"Thanks for the cup o' joe. I'll be in touch."

Dr. Wyatt walked Chief Cutlit out to his cruiser, and watched as his taillights slowly faded into the distance as he drove away. The MOL was parked approximately seventy yards from the beach; he could not see the ocean, but could hear the waves coming ashore.

He knew exactly what he should tell the Chief. He did not want anyone to be killed; it was just too dangerous to take a chance. He shivered as a chill ran up his spine. The darkness of night swallowed him up as he stared out into the pitch black; he felt completely alone and helpless. It was times like these that he missed having someone to lean on. A sick pain grew in his stomach as he struggled for answers.

"I hope Dr. Paige can shed some light on this mystery."

CHAPTER ELEVEN

The waters darkened once more with the coming of night, but that made little difference to these ruthless creatures. They did not rely on sight as much as they did the sense of smell and their ability to detect electromagnetic energy emitted by either animal or machine. Their senses were highly evolved and acute in these waters. They were supreme, the dominant factor, top of the food chain. Nothing they had confronted in this new underworld had any chance of survival. They were unstoppable. Nothing they came across was shown mercy, and all were eliminated from existence with extreme precision.

Their swift forward motion had slowed somewhat; possibly they had finally exhausted their energy, or perhaps they were just saving it up for their next victim. Of course, it was the latter. As the humming vibrations of a motor beckoned, their senses instinctually came to life as they honed in on their next hunt.

CHAPTER TWELVE

Blissfully mesmerized, Dr. Wyatt grinned as Dr. Paige studied the whale specimens, a little pucker between her perfectly manicured eyebrows revealing her absorption in the process. Her professionalism and intellect were top-notch, and Dr. Wyatt already had a strong fascination for her phenomenal body of work. He was a fan, to say the least.

It did not take him long to realize he was also drawn to her as a woman. She was slightly taller than most of the women he knew, not quite eye to eye with him, and she had a way of looking squarely at people that was almost too direct. However, when she opened her mouth, although blunt and to the point, she spoke with such a smooth and gentle sounding Australian accent it destroyed any illusion of severity. She was an enigma—on the one hand hard as nails, and on the other sweet as honey.

Watching Dr. Paige as she paced the floor flipping through paperwork, Kurt's mind raced with unanswered questions— was she married? Single? It was impossible to believe she was not already taken. But if that were the case, could she ever be interested in someone like him? The ends of her straight auburn hair brushed playfully over her shoulders and smelled faintly floral. The unexpected scent made him catch his breath in surprise as she leaned across the table to set the file in front of him. He had not noticed the way a woman smelled since he lost his wife.

Turning his gaze toward his desk, he smiled fondly at the framed photo sitting prominently on his desk. He felt slightly guilty for even thinking of another woman, even though he knew Miranda would not want him to be alone for the rest of his life; she would want him to be happy.

"Kurt? Kurt! KURT!" Dr. Paige brought Dr. Wyatt sharply back to the real world with a thud. His cheeks were tinged bright red as he realized he had been indulging in a romantic daydream the entire time she had been calling his name.

These schoolboy feelings would have to take a back seat for he had more important business to tend to.

"Yes, Amanda?"

"I just don't understand this. It's just like you said, it doesn't match up with anything I have ever seen before. The intensity and savagery of the attacks remind me of a school of starving piranha. One thing I'm reasonably sure of, these are not piranha. I honestly think you may have discovered a new species of shark. But, these sharks are like no other sharks known to man. To prey upon a pod of Orcas and to slaughter them all…" she paused. "I'm at a loss! I have never been so unsure about anything in all my life."

"Think of the devastation they could exert on the oceanographic world, not to mention the very real possibility of them attacking humans. Where could they have come from anyway?" Kurt added his own concerns.

"You're correct, and your guess is as good as mine," Amanda paused thoughtfully. "I would like to send some specimens to my lab in Sydney." Her stern eyes and heightened cheekbones conveyed her importance.

"Sure. I can arrange for that. I sent Shane back to the university for additional research, but he should be getting back soon and he can take care of that for you."

"Thanks, I'd like to go out to sea tonight and see what we can turn up. Is that possible?" Her eyes met his again, and he noticed they lingered a little longer than necessary, but as she looked away he decided it must have been just wishful thinking.

"Yes, most definitely. I need to call Chief Cutlit first though," Kurt smiled and nodded his head in agreement.

CHAPTER THIRTEEN

"It's been hours, and still nothing. I think we'd better head back!" Dr. Wyatt shouted up to Shane as he shielded his eyes from the setting sun.

"Your wish is my command!" Shane spoke with a tongue-in-cheek genie's voice, laughing wickedly as he spun the boat around and roared the engines forward. Shane Briggs had worked under Dr. Wyatt for two years now. He was the doctor's protégé and finest student. Dr. Wyatt secretly hoped some day he would pass the torch to Shane and his work would continue.

"We're heading back! Okay?" Kurt bellowed above the roar of the engine to Amanda.

"Sure. It's been a long day!" Amanda yelled back.

"Let's go below!"

Kurt motioned for Amanda to go down the stairs. As she passed by him, he caught her sweet scent again. It was intoxicating and the butterflies in his stomach seemed to lift him off his feet in her wake. He was definitely attracted to Amanda, but he dared show it. It had been so long since he had these types of feelings; he would not even know where to begin. There was also the fact that it would be terribly unprofessional. They had work to do, and he was sure she was not interested in him anyway.

"Kurt, I'm very impressed with your ship. It's so well equipped. The university must place a high level of interest in your studies."

"Thank you! No complaints here," Kurt replied. "The Malangus is state-of-the-art and the university has always supported the efforts of my department. They fund just about anything I ask for—within reason, of course."

The sounds of the sonar and other equipment could be heard as they reached the bottom of the stairs. Shane radioed the Coast Guard for a status report and learned they had turned up nothing on the missing persons.

"Hmm, I just don't know," Amanda said, visibly worried about those who were missing, especially the young boys. *The sooner we get to the bottom of this the better*, she thought. She felt terrible for them and their families, and she felt guilty at the fact that she was very intrigued and excited over this new discovery.

The rhythmic bouncing of the boat as it cut its way through the choppy water and the fact that she was both mentally and physically exhausted lulled Amanda's thoughts into a drowsy state. She stared in Kurt's direction while he was busy studying the navigational equipment. His knowledge and tireless dedication to his career was impressive, but she was surprised to find that he was equally impressively pleasant to look at. His six-foot stature, athlete's physique, and broad shoulders made him quite a catch for the women around him, to be sure. His tousled, sandy blonde hair that was brushed straight back, his smile with deep dimples on either side, and those sky blue eyes would catch the eye of just about any female, which in Amanda's mind was a problem.

Her thoughts diverted to her ex-boyfriend, whom she once had loved. He had never understood the importance of her career and he was another one that was very easy on the eyes—too good looking to be trusted. She had not discovered his cheating ways until it was too late, and they'd had a blow out breakup. It had been over a year and a half though, and it was time to move on, she thought. But even as her eyes centered on Kurt, she knew this was not a good idea. He turned to face her and they stared at one another timidly, each blushing slightly before looking away.

A feeling of awkwardness filled the room. *Beep! Beep! Beep!* The silence was shattered as the sonar came to life. Amanda bounced up from her chair and joined Kurt as they viewed the sonar monitor.

"Dr. Wyatt?" Shane's voice was heard over the intercom system. He had been watching the sonar from his location above.

Kurt reached over and grabbed the mike. "Go ahead, Shane," Kurt anticipated his question and answered without waiting. "Pursue, but this will be the last one this evening."

"Aye, Cap'n," Shane's voice crackled over the speaker.

Approximately fifteen dots could be seen from the monitor, but they began to rhythmically rise above the water and then descended over and over. The numbers grew as Shane caught up with them. The speed of these creatures and their movements could only lead to one conclusion.

"Looks like dolphins or porpoises," Amanda sighed.

"Yep, that's what it looks like," Kurt agreed, aggravated as he rubbed his forehead in frustration.

"Doctor, looks like a false alarm. Would you like me to head back?" Shane's voice broke through, startling them.

"Yes, I knew it would be like looking for a needle in a haystack." Kurt shook his head.

The boat turned around and increased in acceleration.

"What are you going to tell Chief Cutlit?" Amanda asked.

"Well, not much more than what I've told him already. It appears to be sharks, but no sharks that are yet known to mankind," Kurt spoke solemnly. "They're probably long gone by now anyway."

Unbeknownst to them, just out of sonar range, the dolphins were not only swimming, but were actively being hunted with choreographed accuracy.

CHAPTER FOURTEEN

It was nearly 4 a.m. as Manny, a Filipino American, checked his aging pocket watch with the large flashlight he held steady in his other hand. It had been a good night of crabbing so far and he was about to call it quits and leave the small Turtle Beach bay that meets the Atlantic. He felt pleased at the thought of the profits he and his family would receive from the night's labors.

His son, Alex, had accompanied him this time. At the tender age of six, Alex was his only child, a daddy's boy who always enjoyed helping his father. His thick black hair was constantly unruly. A comb would do little to change his appearance. He was unusually stocky for a boy his age and he handled himself well in the water. Manny knew it was late for a boy his age to be out, but school was not in session, and he did not get to take him crabbing that often.

He stared proudly at the silhouette of his son in the darkness. He knew he was well on his way to becoming a man. A quietness fell upon them. The kind of quiet only a father and son could share; it simply meant that all was right with the world. Manny enjoyed these moments. He seemed to always do better at night, and this night was no different. He and Alex were left alone, with no interference from other fishermen, at his favorite spot to catch crabs.

He had eight large stakes driven deeply into the wet sand with approximately ten yards of nylon string to which an entire raw chicken drumstick was tied to each. The lines were thrown out and slowly dragged back in as Manny scooped them up with his net, snatching the unfortunate crabs from the sea. He also threw a larger net into the waters and pulled in small amounts of crabs, fish, and squid. They had bagged well over a hundred crabs and some fish, which he would sell to the local markets and restaurants at a meager profit. Some, however, he saved to take back for the family to consume. The work provided for his family in an honest and simple way.

Alex's job was to pull the baited strings in while his father did the rest. He took the job of pulling in the bait very seriously and enjoyed the fact that he was assisting his father in putting food on the table. Sweat trickled slowly down the young boy's face as he arduously tugged at the lines and anxiously waited to see what was at the other end.

Manny scooped up several crabs with his net, threw the bait back into the bay, and took their catch over to put in one of ten white buckets that lined the shoreline.

"Papa, is this our last round?" Alex asked in a slightly hopeful voice.

"Sure buddy. I think we're both tired, and you've worked very hard tonight," Manny said proudly as he turned to his son and noticed him yawning, quickly instigating a gaping yawn from him, as well.

He emptied his net in the bucket and headed back to the line, which his son slowly drew in. As usual, Alex had gone into the sea about knee deep to get closer to the action. Manny was about ten yards away from Alex when something caught his eye. He quickly swung his flashlight in that direction. With amazing velocity, every stake that held the string of crab bait was yanked almost simultaneously from the sand and whipped fiercely into the quiet ocean bay. He stared in disbelief, paralyzed in fear. He did not know what to think or do. He had never seen anything like that before in his life. Then a thought hit him! He quickly scanned for his son. "Alex!" he screamed.

He shined the light directly at Alex, who had no idea what was going on. For that matter, neither did Manny. Alex turned to his father, smiling as Manny raced toward his precious son. He had no idea what was out there, but instinct told him that it was death.

"Get out of the water!" Manny screamed frantically, but faster than he could react the string sliced through his son's hands like a razor. He cried out in agony as the stake flashed by his waist, just missing him.

In a flash, the water surrounding the small boy came horribly to life. Alex was seized and effortlessly yanked underwater. Manny, watching from afar screamed wildly and dove headfirst into the evil that lurked below the surface to save his dear son's life. But it was hopeless, for the unforgiving creatures that thirsted for his demise quickly besieged him. Just as he was able to grab his son's arm, the vile forces surged and pulsated from all sides, making it impossible for him to control his own body and Alex was tragically pulled from his father's grip. The water erupted violently as the thrashing beasts' quest for blood was temporarily abated.

Manny had little time to react or feel sorrow, for he was instantly seized by the buttocks and brutally pulled out into deeper water. He had no control over the circumstances as he was savagely ripped apart, limb from limb. Shredded lumps of unrecognizable flesh and splintered bone floated aimlessly through the murky water. In an instant, Manny and his son assumed their place at the bottom of the food chain as the new top predators of the ocean instinctually consumed all evidence, leaving no proof of their existence and no one to carry on the victims' family name.

As quickly as the attack began, it was over. A fingernail shaped slice of the moon peered ominously through a cloud break and was quickly covered again. An eerie silence enveloped the darkness as a cool breeze swept lightly across the bay. A single crab managed to climb from its bucket, scurrying sideways to return to the now bloodied sea.

CHAPTER FIFTEEN

Kurt awoke confused as he reached over, with sight still blurry, and angrily pressed the snooze button on his loud alarm clock. But the ringing persisted.

"What on earth?" he muttered, his head waging a silent battle between sleep and wakefulness. *Ugh, it's the phone.* Finally finding his bearings as the fog gradually released his sight, he rolled off the side of the bed, glancing over to his clock on his way to the phone. *It's only 4:30!*

Kurt groaned in pain as his knee caught the corner of the cabinet a few feet away from his bed. He hobbled to the phone as his heart rate rose; a call at this hour could only mean bad news.

"Hello!" Kurt answered the phone, clutching his knee and aiming a death glare at the cabinet as if this would somehow relieve the throbbing in his knee. He noticed Amanda enter from the next room and he watched as she flipped on the light. She looked like a little girl that had just been woken up for school. Her hair, normally perfectly styled, was in disarray, strands dangling in front of her squinting eyes. Her rumpled lavender nightshirt attested to the fact that she too had been woken too abruptly. The throbbing in his knee was quickly forgotten in the presence of her sleepy innocence.

"Dr. Wyatt?" a familiar voice could be heard over the line, "It's Chief Cutlit."

"Yes, what is it?" Dr. Wyatt answered, sensing the urgency in the Chief's voice.

"You and Dr. Paige might want to get over to the Turtle Beach Marina right away. The Coast Guard has found one of the jet skis— or what's left of it at least. It looks bad, pretty much mangled, and there's still no sign of the missing boys."

"We'll be right there," Kurt hung up the phone and offered an explanation to Amanda. "We have to go to the marina. The Coast Guard has recovered one of the jet skis. Chief Cutlit said it was in pretty bad shape."

"What about the boys?" Amanda anxiously asked.

"Nothing. No sign," Kurt frowned, shrugging his shoulders.

Neither one said another word as they turned toward their rooms to get dressed and prepared to go.

In his room, Kurt tiredly scrubbed his hands over his face as he tried to process the day before him. As tired as he had been the night before, he'd had trouble falling asleep. He was very aware that Amanda was sleeping just in the next room. They were alone in the MOL, for he'd sent Shane back to the university for lab work and to pick up needed supplies and equipment. Kurt recognized that he felt the spark of new feelings for Amanda. Every time he was around her, his stomach felt brutally empty and his mouth became dry. However, he was not the kind of man that allowed himself to fall in love indiscriminately. He needed to take things slowly and truly get to know her—a hard thing to do when your heart reacted on its own volition. When he had finally managed to drift off to sleep, his dreams played tug-of-war between the sharks and Amanda.

In her own room, Amanda stared at herself in the mirror while she brushed her teeth. She looked rough this morning, and she knew it. In her mind, it was probably good that Kurt had seen her like this. She had noticed the way he looked at her when he thought her attention was elsewhere. Even though Kurt seemed different than other men, more trustworthy and dependable, she was still unsure whether she was ready to care for or trust another man. He had looked really good though, with his hair all standing on end as he rubbed the sleep out of his eyes, but she pushed that image out of her mind. It would be incredibly awkward to work with him if she lingered on these thoughts, and she knew there were more important things to deal with right now.

CHAPTER SIXTEEN

The light of day broke over the horizon and the sun blanketed the ocean's surface with reddish-orange warmth, leaving behind the sterility of night and ushering in the new day. The creatures swam with powerful, effortless grace, cutting through the waters before them. Genetically programmed over thousands of years, their instinctual need to kill forever burned deep within them. Their hunger was insatiable and in this new world the prey was plentiful.

Their senses sharpened, miles away they could sense the buzzing and splashing of potential prey. Swiftly turning and advancing in that direction with a single-purposed exactness, they represented a well-trained team. Each was well aware of the others' positions in formation as they torpedoed into battle. The hatred distended and their speed gradually increased to twenty-five miles an hour, their stalking speed. They could swim as fast as forty miles an hour in short bursts. There was no escaping these beasts. No animal of the ocean stood a chance against these awesome killing machines. They were the epitome of evolutionary perfection—bound and determined for the hunt, their thirst for slaughter ever increasing. Miles away, the unsuspecting prey unknowingly waited—its fate already determined.

CHAPTER SEVENTEEN

"Dr. Paige, Dr. Wyatt, this is Captain Lucas of the U.S. Coast Guard," Chief Cutlit cordially introduced the parties and gracefully stepped aside.

Captain Lucas stood sternly before his two guests with an ancient soggy cigar that looked like it had never been lit clenched tightly between his teeth. His aged, leathery face and gray hair perfectly captured the story of his hard life at sea. He was a respected man with thirty-five years of service, and in all of those years he had never witnessed such a spectacle. He was completely dumbfounded.

"Good morning, Doctors," Captain Lucas said, his gruff and commanding voice befitting his weathered look.

"Good morning, Captain. Let's see what you have here, sir," Amanda said anxiously.

They made their way onto the U.S.C.G. Ulysses and maneuvered toward the bow through the bustle of the ship's crew. Considering it was 5:30 in the morning, it was amazing to observe the U.S. Coast Guard officers diligently working all about the ship, each tending to their own specific tasks while officers bellowed out orders. To Amanda, the men appeared to harmoniously move to a perfectly scripted and graceful dance, kept in time to music only the sailors could hear.

"Here we are," proclaimed Captain Lucas as a few of his men lifted the canvas from the tattered and barely recognizable Jet Ski.

Amanda and Kurt carefully surveyed the evidence that lay before them for several minutes while Captain Lucas and Chief Cutlit casually expressed their own conclusions on how the jet ski came to its current condition. The Jet Ski looked as if a hammer had beaten every inch. The paint had been almost completely scoured off and the handlebars and seat cushion were mangled and torn to shreds.

Amanda was first to break the silence, speaking more to herself than anyone else in an almost inaudible voice, "This is undeniably the work of a shark, and not just one, but many. What doesn't add up is the frequency and the force behind each impact."

"How can you be sure those dents and scrapes aren't from the reef or chewed up by a cruise ship?" Chief Cutlit interrupted.

Kurt stood up, looked cautiously toward Amanda and then to the other men. "I have to agree with Dr. Paige. I've never seen anything even remotely like this. Its sharks all right... the bite patterns in the fiberglass and hoses, and the scrapes caused by a shark's sandpaper-like skin are evidence to that."

"Chief, I think you have enough justification to call off this tournament. It's imperative that we get to the bottom of this," Amanda's rattled voice declared. She was scared, yet excited at the notion of a new species of shark in the sea—something completely new to the world of science.

"I understand that, but unfortunately the competition has already begun." the Chief's eyes widened.

"This early in the morning?" Kurt asked incredulously, squinting at his wristwatch. "How many are entered in the contest?"

"Enough."

Amanda and Kurt simultaneously looked into one another's eyes to see the urgency and fear of the unknown, which they both shared. There would be far too much activity in the area for these creatures not to gravitate towards. They quickly realized the real danger the situation created.

Chief Cutlit took his radio from his belt and put it to his mouth "Unit 103...105..."

As the Chicf radioed his officers to close the beach, six coast guard officers loaded the damaged jet ski in the back of Kurt's Jeep Cherokee. Further tests would need to be performed before the original assessment of the two young doctors could be validated.

"Don't worry. We'll clear the waters," announced Captain Lucas.

Amanda and Kurt nearly raced to the Jeep. As they backed up, Kurt came to a stop beside Chief Cutlit's cruiser. The Chief had just finished his conversation on his radio, and he looked almost helplessly over at Kurt, the gravity of the situation finally sinking in.

"Amanda and I are heading out to sea to look for anything we can possibly turn up. Contact us by radio if you need us."

"Sure, my men are closing the beach as we speak, and I'm heading over to the tournament right now. I'll catch up with you later." The Chief pulled away quickly, lights flashing and tires squealing.

Kurt followed in the chief's wake. As he drove away, he glanced in his rear view mirror to see that the U.S.C.G. Ulysses had already set off on its mission.

CHAPTER EIGHTEEN

All one hundred and thirty-four competitors had already set sail into the tranquil blue-green sea on the quest to become the Turtle Beach International Pro-Spearfishing Tournament Champion. All charted different courses, some having scientifically calculated their destination, while others went on instinct alone. This was a nationally recognized tournament with top-notch competitors, ages ranging anywhere between sixteen to seventy-two years old.

Chunga welcomed the exhilaration of the cool water and the surge of adrenaline as he dove from his two-man fishing boat. He liked this spot, he thought to himself as he resurfaced for a breath. He had put considerable distance between himself and the others, and could not see any fishermen close-by. He liked it that way. He had ventured further down the coastline to a spot he had a hunch would produce. He was a man of chance and, as was his nature, he took quite a few of them. You had to be a little crazy to participate in this sport, and Chunga did not disappoint. He had once speared a barracuda at the end of a dive, something others would not even attempt, let alone succeed at.

Using quick jerky motions, Chunga shook his head to get the water out of his face as he reached into the boat for his gear. Unlike the long lean lines of others that swam for either fortune or entertainment, Chunga's physical characteristics were different than most that participated in this sport. At over six feet tall and carrying more than a little extra weight, his pudgy middle gave him the silhouette of a harp seal. Unfortunately for those that dismissed him as true competition, he could also hold his breath and swim like one.

Chunga was ready to get busy. He had just started to descend when a movement in the distance caught his eye. His momentum carried him downward, but with the rapid movement of his fins he easily propelled upward again. Resurfacing, he jerked his mask from his head and hurriedly looked in every direction, his eyes sharply focusing on the danger before him. The sea fell silent, the only sound audible to Chunga was the beating of the blood to his temples. One hundred and fifty yards away, a hideous dark mass swiftly approached him, moving like lightning. Normally, he did not scare easily, but Chunga could see a legion of fins heading directly towards him and he was nervous.

Dolphins? Or... sharks! It has to be sharks!

None of the creatures broke through the water for air as they bee-lined directly toward him as if they were guided by GPS. The sheer number of them had Chunga fumbling behind himself for the safety of his boat, only to find it was not there. It had drifted considerably.

He frantically swam the distance between him and the boat, chopping at the water uncharacteristically from fear. It felt like he swam for miles before he was able to reach out and grab his boat. He failed at his first attempt at boarding the craft, falling short as he splashed back into the water.

The dark mass grew ever closer and Chunga felt the pressure of their presence almost upon him. Finally, with a heave and a grunt, the thirty year old flung himself resolutely into the boat. Gasping for breath, he turned around hoping his unwelcome visitors had disappeared, but he was not that lucky. Heading straight for him with a single-minded purpose that made his skin crawl were the predators.

His heart sank into the pit of his stomach, feeling three times its size as a cold numbness consumed his entire body. Shivering uncontrollably, he realized for the first time in his life he was scared, and he did not like the feeling. Pulling and tugging the anchor up from the ocean's floor with all his might, he kept a close eye on the creatures as they swam closer and closer.

I've never seen a jagged-shaped fin like that on any shark before. It's not normal, he thought as he pulled the anchor aboard his shabby fishing boat. He scrambled for the outboard motor and pushed the ignition button, begging, "Please start this time! Just this once...START!"

The old engine sputtered for a few seconds and fell silent. "Come on, you piece of junk!" he screamed before remembering to prime the gas. He pumped it three times and tried the ignition button again. The engine then rumbled to life.

"Yes!" Chunga yelled triumphantly. Unexpectedly, he was jolted to the front of the boat, "Whaaaa?" he screeched, tumbling forward. Well aware of what had hit the boat, he had been caught off-guard for their speed was deceptive.

Scrambling frantically for the engine, he grabbed the steering and gunned the accelerator toward the beach. His small craft was violently hit again, but this time he held fast, staying steady on his feet. He took a chance looking down to his attackers and his eyes froze in panic. The savage creatures that craved his flesh glared at him with their emotionless, cold black eyes as their gaping jaws of death lay waiting just below the water's surface. Chunga only had a slim chance to get away, but it was sadly diminishing with every second. He had the engine at full throttle and the beasts were still effortlessly keeping up with him.

Just ahead, other boats came into view.

"Help! Help! Somebody help me!" Chunga screamed, but the other divers could not hear him. They were on their own underwater quest for the prized catch and title.

He felt another bump against the hull and looked back. In that split second, one of the sharks raised its head out of the water, and its mouth, almost completely obstructed with hideous, jagged teeth, clamped down on the middle section of the boat. It spun around as it jack-knifed and flipped over, sending Chunga end over end into the feeding frenzy. It was over the second he hit the water.

A pair of jaws clamped down across his stomach opening his entire midsection, gruesomely disemboweling him. Still alive, in the last pitiable seconds of Chunga's life, all he could do was scream helplessly. The waters frothed tumultuously red as the sharks hungrily feasted on their prey.

Chunga was quickly completely devoured, and then the ocean returned to a superficial calm—hiding the evil that lurked below. The idling engine of the empty boat muffled and gurgled and eventually extinguished as the old rickety craft slowly sank to the depths below, covering all traces of the recent carnage.

Yet still, the hunger was not abated.

CHAPTER NINETEEN

"Malangus, come in! Dr. Wyatt, do you read me? This is Chief Cutlit."

Kurt reached over and grabbed the mike, "Chief Cutlit. Dr. Wyatt here; over."

"Dr. Wyatt, we received another missing persons report. Two professional spear fishermen, last seen yesterday, are now missing." Chief Cutlit's voice crackled over the radio.

"I'm sorry to hear about that, Chief." Kurt looked at Amanda, shaking his head with regret. He frowned slightly, clearly seeing the signs of stress and concern in her eyes at the news.

"I just wanted to be sure you were aware that we, in conjunction with the Coast Guard, are in the process of warning all divers and spectators to clear the waters immediately."

"That's good. We're nearing the site of the tournament. I think you know the urgency of getting everyone out of the water. These sharks are just looking for an opportunity like this. If you need any assistance on land, contact my assistant, Shane, back at the mobile lab."

"Sure thing, and if anything turns up on your end..." Chief Cutlit paused abruptly. "No! It's too late! Get them out..."

The line went dead. Amanda and Kurt looked wide-eyed at one another, and then to the disturbingly tranquil sea before them.

"Chief Cutlit! Chief Cutlit, come in! Chief!" Kurt shouted into the radio.

"It's too late. They're already there!" Amanda whispered.

Kurt did not respond, except to slam the mike back into its cradle and shift the motor into full throttle towards the tournament site.

CHAPTER TWENTY

Chief Cutlit was terror-stricken as he spied through his binoculars the multitude of sharks literally devouring boats and unfortunate competitors as they struggled for the sanctuary of the beach. Everything in their path was completely ripped apart or consumed. The chief's men did all they could to get everyone out of the water, but it was just not good enough. The swarm had overwhelmed the gathering. The Coast Guard made their way toward the massacre, warning the people further up the coastline to get out of the water.

A sailor's voice boomed over a bullhorn, "CLEAR THE WATER!"

Cutlit's men had already cleared the spectators and swimmers from the beach and were assisting those fortunate enough to crawl from the jaws of death before they collapsed exhausted at the waters edge. Cutlit dropped his binoculars in the sand where he stood and ran frantically to help.

Corporal Johnstone, in all the commotion and chaos, had heroically swam fifty yards out to save two female competitors who had accidentally turned over their small craft and were swimming for shore, though not making enough headway. Chief Cutlit could see there was not much hope Johnstone would make it to them in time. Even if he did, it would likely be futile. The sharks were fast approaching.

"Johnstone!" The chief screamed. Not thinking twice about what he was risking, he busted through the waves and dove in head first to help his friend.

"Hhhheellggghhh!"

Johnstone heard the ladies' gurgled screams as he grew closer. He was within an arm's length when they both grabbed onto Johnstone, their death grips preventing him from swimming and pulling him down. He could see the terror in their eyes as he struggled to stay afloat.

"Calm downgghh... " Johnstone gasped for air as he went under. "We have to work together. Lets go!" He went under again. "We have to swiggghh!" Swallowing mouthfuls of seawater, Johnstone uselessly pleaded for them to calm down. In their panic, they pulled him under, making matters worse. They were so scared that all they did was hang on for dear life.

With a burst of furious kicking from his legs, fueled by pure adrenaline, Johnstone surfaced again only to stare wide-eyed directly into the gaping jaws of death. They were here, right on top of him!

The water surrounding the small group convulsed and pulsated as the creatures grew excited by the frenzy about to take place. One of the girls was ripped from his grasp, and Johnstone screamed as she was torn apart right in front of him.

In the quickly fading seconds of his life, he tried desperately to swim from this living nightmare. He managed only one stroke before serrated teeth clamped down between his legs and groin, his right calf, and then his neck. He felt the jarring impacts of each attack, screaming as the bones crunched and muscle was ripped from his body. Mercifully, the light from his eyes quickly extinguished and his life ended.

"Noooooo! Please no!" Cutlit cried out, watching in horror as the three were slaughtered right before his eyes. The panic-filled waters surrounding him turned his thoughts swiftly to his own predicament. Would he make it back to shore alive? Was this the end for him?

He turned back and began to swim for his life. The shoreline looked far too distant and he knew every second counted. He did not dare even glance back, but focused all his attention on taking long smooth strokes back to the safety of the shore. His days as a lifeguard on this very same beach many years ago flashed before his eyes. How young and naïve he had been—believing in his own immortality, never dreaming anything like this could ever truly happen. A sudden burst of adrenaline hit him and he gave it his all, surging ahead, mere seconds before he felt something grab him. His shriek of terror could be heard up and down the beach.

"Chief, are you all right?" Voices shot from all directions, confusing him as he was dragged quickly from the water. He lay on the beach for a moment, soaked with seawater and sucking in great gulps of air before he realized he had made it out alive.

Wiping salt water from his eyes, he strained to see only remnants of boats, debris, and the Coast Guard's Ulysses still announcing over loud speakers for people to clear the water. *Good timing*, he thought angrily to himself, but he knew they had done all they could.

Hearing the victim's screams over and over in his head, along with the memories of those hideous jagged fins flashing through his mind changed something fundamental within him. It lit a burning fire in his very soul for vengeance.

CHAPTER TWENTY-ONE

"Oh my! Kurt, look!" Amanda quickly turned to Kurt with a look of fear blanketing her now pale face.

Kurt stood paralyzed, temporarily losing his ability to speak. Scattered pieces of boats and debris littered the water before them. The beach itself was in utter chaos. People ran in all directions in the midst of flashing lights and sirens from the emergency vehicles as the Coast Guard crews hurriedly pulled as many people as they could from the water. The commotion surrounding Kurt seemed strangely distant and muffled, as if filtered through an unseen barrier. His mind became numb at what he witnessed.

Beep! Beep! Beep! The sonar came to life, jerking Kurt back to reality.

"Prepare yourself. They're heading straight for us!" Kurt said, trying unsuccessfully to hide his mounting anxiety.

"They're what?" Amanda asked, knowing already she had heard him correctly.

Wide-eyed, Amanda and Kurt stared down at the hideously dark mass rapidly approaching the Malangus. The prominent jagged fins and their pitch-black color amazed the two scientists. It was absolutely mystifying. Horrified and panic stricken, they were still humbled at the fact they were among the very few who had ever witnessed nature's most efficient killing machines. Kurt's thoughts were jumbled, but he knew he had to do something, and the first thing was to save the as many as they could from these methodical monsters. He did not have enough weapons for that number of sharks, or even the time to prepare them if he had, for that matter.

"Turn the boat around and let them chase us! There's no way they can keep pace with us for very long," Amanda said, more to reassure herself than anything else.

Not saying a word, Kurt did exactly as he was told. He whipped the ship around, throttled the engine, and headed for the far horizon, praying the predators would follow. He deliberately tried not to lose his pursuers; he could not afford to. He had to lead them away from the tournament, hoping against all odds that they would be able to save at least one more person.

Several minutes passed and still the beasts were keeping a steady pace with the Malangus.

"This is unreal," Kurt yelled in amazement above the roar of the boat's engine. *Unbelievable*, he thought to himself. The adrenaline rush of witnessing a creature yet to be identified by science, and its amazing abilities, was clearly visible on Kurt's face.

In the back of his mind, he knew if they were somehow able to capture and study one of these previously unknown sharks, it would be quite beneficial for him. Not only would it put him at the top of the oceanographic world, it would also mean he would be able to spend more time with Amanda. However, right now, vanity and personal accolades would have to wait.

"I'm going below to turn on our underwater cameras. I know it's probably a lost cause since the boat is mobile, but we have nothing to lose and the world to gain," Amanda shouted into the wind.

"All right," said Kurt, his head whipping back and forth between the sonar in front of him to the sharks behind him. He turned one of his deck video cameras slightly and panned in on the sharks. He needed to gather as much evidence about them as possible. The sophisticated equipment onboard the Malangus made it that much easier, but he knew, as well as Amanda did, they needed an actual specimen. *How do we catch one of these bad boys?* he thought.

"Malangus, come in," Chief Cutlit's voice crackled over the radio. Kurt quickly reached for the mike.

"This is the Malangus. Go ahead, Chief."

"As you're probably aware, those devils killed a lot of people! Do you know where they are now? They've disappeared."

"I sure do, Chief! They're right on our tail! We're leading them out to sea, away from the beaches!"

"Good thinking. As soon as the Coast Guard is finished here, I'll be on my way to kill every last one of 'em! If there's any way you can take out some in the meantime, do it!"

"I'll do what I can, but I don't have much artillery on board," Kurt hesitantly agreed before hanging up the mike. Kurt knew anger was getting the best of the normally docile Chief Cutlit, and he could not blame him. He and Amanda needed to quickly gather as much information as possible on these dangerous, but beautifully magnificent creatures, before any foolish actions were taken, only to be regretted later.

"Did you see anything on the underwater cams?"

"Nothing but a blur," Amanda said breathlessly, as she reached the top of the stairs.

"Amanda, could you take over the controls? I need to check on our firepower. Or should I say lack of firepower?"

"Sure, we need to take every precaution necessary." Amanda took her position at the helm, while Kurt went below to sift through the equipment compartments.

"Don't they ever get tired?" Amanda hissed under her breath. Her desire to stop the Malangus and study these oddities was equal to Kurt's. They could not chance it, however, for they had both witnessed the awesome power and fatal destruction left in their wake. More importantly, she recognized they needed to lead them as far away from people as possible and, accordingly, she adjusted their course for the furthest point on the horizon.

CHAPTER TWENTY-TWO

They had flourished in their hunt, but now some were starting to show signs of fatigue. Several had gotten close, only to barely nick the large water creature that noisily moved before them. Sparked by this new formidable challenger they tirelessly pressed on. Although they had eaten well only minutes before, they hungered for a fresh kill. The rage and excitement flowed through them for this rival could possibly be the most worthy opponent yet.

CHAPTER TWENTY-THREE

"I can't believe they're still keeping up with us!" Amanda yelled as she stood on the deck of the boat looking up to Kurt, her hair whipping in the wind. She could tell he was not paying any attention. He was too busy fiddling with the ship's controls. She could sense by Kurt's jumbled and hurried actions something was wrong. Without hesitation, Amanda bolted to his side.

"Kurt, what is it?"

"I don't know what's wrong with this bloomin' thing! Just look at this," Kurt implored. Bewildered, they examined the sonar's video screen, which displayed absolutely nothing resembling sonar activity. The beeping sounds from the sonar were also erratic and incomprehensible. Kurt did everything possible to rectify the problem to no avail.

"Maybe it's a computer glitch," Amanda suggested. "But wait! Take a look at this!"

Kurt's eyebrows rose in disbelief at what she pointed to. "Oh, this is too much!" Kurt and Amanda stared at the compass in amazement as it whirled out of control.

"A compass doesn't need electricity to work, so what's the problem?" Amanda's cool as a cucumber exterior was beginning to show signs that the situation was becoming too stressful.

"All I know is that it picked a bad time to stop working. Amanda, I need to go below and check the other equipment. Can you take the controls again and just keep this pace? Those things can't possibly keep up with us forever."

Kurt almost slid down the ladder before his feet firmly struck the deck, causing his teeth to smack together painfully. He sprinted for the next set of stairs to go below. He was about halfway down when he remembered the sharks. He raced back up the stairs, shading his eyes nervously as he scanned the area encompassing the Malangus.

"Where'd they go?" Kurt stared in disbelief as he brought the bottom of his oxford shirt up to his face to wipe the sweat away. There was nothing—not a menacing fin in sight. But that did not necessarily mean they were gone. "Oh no, they're trying to outsmart us," Kurt mumbled under his breath in a moment of realization. Kurt looked up to Amanda, also scanning feverishly for the creatures, when their eyes unexpectedly met. They had both come to the same conclusion.

Amanda motioned downward, letting Kurt know she believed they had submerged. Kurt nodded in agreement and scurried below. His thoughts were briefly of Amanda's safety, but he had to force himself to concentrate on the problems at hand.

As Kurt reached the bottom step and paused momentarily to catch his breath, he could hear the sonar's erratic beeping, as well as the printer's high-pitched screeching. Upon entering the control room, he found all of the electronic equipment going haywire. Turning off the printer and the volume to the sonar, he looked for a problem with the computer system. He could not help but to glare angrily at the computer monitor, it too was experiencing technical difficulties. The screen was alive with numerical and alphabetical gibberish, the characters smearing across the screen and then fading into nothingness.

"C'mon!" Kurt yelled as he firmly struck the side of the CPU with his palm, angrily reprimanding the inanimate object.

So much for state-of-the-art.

Kurt shifted his gaze toward the underwater video monitors, but before his eyes could reach their destination the power to everything, including the ship, went down. He stood motionless in the quiet darkness. As he waited patiently for his eyes to adjust, his hearing became his primary sense. He tilted his head slightly, as if this action could somehow improve his hearing, and listened intently, but only the swell of the ocean's waves caused by the momentum of the ship's forward progress pierced the lonely stillness.

"Kurt? Get up here now!" The seriousness of Amanda's voice cut through the darkness.

CHAPTER TWENTY-FOUR

"Dr. Wyatt, come in!" Captain Lucas shouted into the mike in irritation. "Dr. Wyatt! This is Captain Lucas of the U.S. Coast Guard Ulysses. Please respond!" Irritating static was all that could be heard by Captain Lucas, Chief Cutlit, and the men on the bridge. The chief hung his head, shaking it slowly from side to side, quietly fearing the worst for the doctors. The Ulysses surged through the waters searching for the Malangus.

"Officer Peters, anything?"

"Nothing, sir," Officer Peters responded.

"It's like they just fell off the face of the planet," Chief Cutlit said, confusion giving way to anger. "I tell you what, this is all poppycock. If I'm dreaming, somebody kick me in the behind and wake me up! An entire boat just doesn't vanish!"

"It is a mystery." Captain Lucas explained, "In all my years at sea, I've never seen the likes of this. I've notified my highest commanding officer, Admiral Norge, and I'm awaiting further orders. We'll continue looking for the Malangus and the sharks, or whatever you say they are, till I'm told otherwise."

Chief Cutlit cut in, "We need to warn others in the area, if it's not already too late."

"I'm sure everyone in the world knows about this by now. All Coast Guard units have been notified, and have alerted the authorities. They're clearing the waters as we speak. We've also had the media's assistance in getting the word out. Don't be surprised when we get back if we see news crews from all the networks, along with other reporters, there to greet us at the docks." Captain Lucas rolled his eyes in dismay.

Chief Cutlit took a big swig of his coffee and cringed in pain as the unexpectedly hot brew burned his tongue. He slowly sat back into his chair and blew out a huff of air. He was physically and mentally drained.

Could I have stopped this from happening, he thought regretfully. *How was I to know?* Staring at the floor, before clutching his head and closing his eyes, he wished it would all go away. But another, deeper part of him needed answers and he needed them now. *What are these monsters and where did they come from?*

CHAPTER TWENTY-FIVE

"We will keep you updated on this horrible tragedy as we learn more. Reporting to you live from Turtle Beach, Florida, this is Tina Hunt."

Admiral Norge muted the television and firmly placed the remote on his grand mahogany desk. He was a highly decorated and hardened man at the age of sixty-one years. He had diligently worked his way up through the ranks where he now held the top post at the U.S. Coast Guard for the last fifteen years. He was very well respected and liked by everyone, including the most recent president, who had given him the appointment as the Commandant of the U.S. Coast Guard. His white hair and bushy eyebrows created a presence of wisdom and experience that blanketed him like an aged cloak. His dark, piercing eyes seemed to harness all the light from the room, and the wrinkles in his face told the story of his adventurous, rugged life at sea. He loudly exhaled air through his nose, expressing his importance and urgency regarding this matter.

"Admiral?"

"Excuse me, sir?" The officer at the door tried once again.

Admiral Norge was abruptly startled from his intense and trance-like thought to see his second-in-command, Admiral Edwards.

"Yes, Edwards?"

"Do you think we should dispatch more ships to that vicinity?"

Admiral Norge paused, spinning his chair slightly to the left to gaze out his window as he pondered Admiral Edwards' question. His chair squeaked as he rocked it slowly back and forth. "I think five of our ships and eight copters are sufficient for the time being. We have the Navy onboard as well. Have Detachment 213 put on alert for possible deployment though, just in case."

"This is all just a freak of nature," Admiral Edwards sheepishly offered as both a question and suggestion, "right?"

"Only God knows, Edwards—and it doesn't look like he's going to fill us in any time soon."

Edwards was somewhat new to his position as Admiral Norge's right-hand man, but he had almost as many years of experience with the Coast Guard.

"We don't know what we're dealing with; that's the problem. You saw the news as surely as I did. Pictures don't lie." The Admiral slowly and purposefully leaned towards Edwards, looking at him square in the eyes with his intense gaze.

"I have never seen sharks like that in all my years at sea," Admiral Norge whispered gruffly, as if he did not want anyone else to hear. "There are no sharks that swim with such uniform exactness in such great numbers, as well as strategically attacking and killing that many people for no apparent reason. None of it makes any sense."

A deafening silence consumed the room as both men contemplated for a moment the implications of the Admiral's statement.

"I agree," Edwards capitulated. "I'm sure Captain Lucas will reestablish contact with the marine biologists and maybe they can shed some light on what we're dealing with. I do know one thing for certain, we need to locate those sharks before they kill again."

"With all the missing persons reports in that area, it looks like this is not an isolated incident. Everything leads back to those sharks. Telling people to stay out of the water is one thing, but you know not everyone will heed those warnings."

"Admiral?" the familiar voice of Ms. Murine, his secretary, urgently intruded over the intercom. Both men looked at one another and then to the phone.

"Yes, Mattie?"

Her voice was shaky and nervous, "The President is on line one. He would like to speak with you immediately, sir."

CHAPTER TWENTY-SIX

"You're not going to believe this, but I think I know why the equipment is malfunctioning. It would explain why we've lost power completely, even to our backups." Kurt sounded fatigued and frustrated at their continuing misfortune.

"Surprise me," Amanda said wryly.

"It's the only answer I can come up with right now," Kurt paused, questioning if he should even suggest something so absurd. But he figured in light of everything that happened lately, anything was possible at this very odd juncture of time.

He could see the concern etched on Amanda's face as dark anticipation hung over her like a storm cloud. Her right eyebrow was raised as she waited for the worst possible news to fall from his lips, almost accepting of their doom before she even heard his explanation. She nervously chewed on her bottom lip, something Kurt had noticed in previous conversations and found endearing.

Shaking his head, he cleared his thoughts, realizing they were in quite a predicament and it was possibly the least appropriate time to let his feelings run away with him. There were too many important concerns—life threatening concerns, at that.

"Well," Kurt paused, feverishly rubbing his forehead with both hands before taking a deep breath and exhaling. "We're in an area known as the Triangle." Kurt was embarrassed these words actually left his mouth. His entire life, every decision or statement he ever made had been based on logical fact. Everything had an explanation. But now he found himself saying—and actually believing—something he used to think was an old sailor's tale. Apprehensively, he found himself looking to Amanda for her reaction.

"The Bermuda Triangle?" Amanda spoke hesitantly, looking puzzled. "Isn't that just superstition?"

"Yes, I believe so. Or at least I once did. I've logged so many hours in this area, the Devil's Triangle, and I'd yet to witness even the slightest anomaly until today."

"Kurt, it's not logical." Amanda's thoughts jumbled and her concentration faltered. "That's right up there with witchcraft and werewolves," she chuckled jokingly.

"I know. Trust me, I know how absurd it sounds. But what else could it be? Even the generator won't give us any juice, and the compass is spinning like a coffee grinder. Maybe there are things in life that just can't be based on logical, scientific fact. Look at the events over the past few days. Answer me honestly. If I had come to you this time last year and told you I had discovered what we now have, wouldn't you have been more than a little skeptical?"

"I suppose so," Amanda conceded softly, an awkward and intense pause filling the air between them.

"Well, at least the Coast Guard should be getting here soon," Amanda said, offering a half-smile and unsuccessfully attempting to change the subject.

"You know," she continued, her eyes sparkling with excitement. "This might be the perfect time to get a little wet and see just what we're actually dealing with here."

"Yeah, I don't think that would be such a good idea. We don't have the electricity to run our equipment, which includes the shark cage. Besides that, you've observed the damage they can do. We would probably be just as safe going down in nothing at all."

"I know, but I'll play it safe and stay near the ship. I'm just going to have a look-see below. I'm curious, but I'm not stupid," she answered, a tight grin on her face.

"No way am I going to let you go below! I'll go," Kurt staunchly volunteered. He wanted more than anything to protect Amanda from any danger.

"Thank you, sir! However, the last time I checked, you were in no position to tell me what I can and cannot do!" Amanda spoke jokingly, but Kurt could tell there was an underlying seriousness in her tone. Gone was the anxious girl of a few moments ago, only to be replaced by a fiery woman unafraid of any challenge.

Amanda had spent years working in her profession. Against all odds, she had fought and clawed her way to the top in a male dominated field, and she had not gotten there by standing by and letting men shield her. Her independence and confidence abruptly halted any argument from Kurt.

"Besides, I need you up top. If you wait by the ladder and warn me at the first sight of any danger, then you can pull me up in a jiffy."

Kurt had been raised to be a gentleman; everything about this struck him as wrong. He felt like someone was twisting his insides and not letting go, but he knew Amanda was a professional. She was more experienced and knowledgeable of sharks, so he reluctantly consented. "Alright, but I'll be right here if you need me."

Amanda disappeared from sight as she headed below to change into scuba gear. Kurt, in the meantime, loaded another flare into the flare gun, pointed upward, and shot it into the sky. The flare surged upward, zigzagging back and forth till it climaxed and burned itself out in a hazy amber glow.

Where are they? He surveyed the water surrounding the Malangus all the way out to the horizon using his binoculars. There was sign of neither sharks nor Coast Guard. Kurt laid the binoculars down within reach and shook his head in irritation.

"I'll bet they're down there... just waiting for us to make our move," Kurt murmured to no one in particular. "Smart fishies!"

Kurt made his way to the storage compartment and readied their tanks and other equipment for the dive. He was also getting suited up. He wanted to be ready, just in case Amanda needed him. For her, he was willing to put himself smack in the middle of danger.

CHAPTER TWENTY-SEVEN

An excited yet terrifying exhilaration rapidly spread to every point in Amanda's body as she broke the surface of the ominous waters. Her eyes widened instantly as she investigated her surroundings as far as she could see.

Nothing! So strange, she thought. Not even a solitary fish was in sight.

With each efficient thrust of her flippers, she continued to swim gracefully downward through the desolate and murky sea. Her survival instincts in high gear, she checked every few seconds on the location of the boat, as well as for the hideous creatures that had already so drastically changed her life.

She had always felt at one with the sea. Even now, with her nerves stretched as tight as a piano wire, it was difficult to determine where her body ended and the waters surrounding her began. Am I stuck in a nightmare? She wondered. But the sound of her breathing apparatus and the pounding of her heart assured her she was unquestionably awake. What she was doing was more than dangerous, but it came with the job. She longed to understand more about what was out there. After all, sharks meant everything to her.

Amanda easily swam to a depth of about two hundred feet when she was abruptly hit from above without warning. She felt an abrupt tightness around her waist. There was no great pain, but she knew when a shark attacked a person they typically did not feel pain, but rather experience a cool, burning sensation where they had been bitten.

She knew these could be her last few moments on earth, and she was not going to go down without a fight. Her heart raced out of rhythm, and the thought of being eaten alive hardened like a stone in her gut. She jolted herself downward, trying to free herself from her unseen attacker, but came to an abrupt stop. Unable to move another inch, she was held steadfast as her captor tightened its grip on her. With no other choice and her insides quaking in fear, she swung around to face her aggressor; again, the grip tightened.

Instant relief blanketed her entire body and she laughed at herself in relief. She had only come to the end of the rope that had been tied to her as a safety precaution. In the case of an emergency, Kurt would have instantly pulled her up and out of danger. Amanda regained her composure and studied the waters around her. She had enough excitement for one dive. There was nothing to be found, no living creature to be seen. None of it made sense.

Was the sea life fearful of these creatures? Where did they all go? These and many other questions cycloned through her investigative mind as she started the long journey back to the safety of the surface, still checking the area and trying to calm herself from her unexpected scare. At least, she had a good story to tell.

Amanda was approximately twenty-five feet from the surface where she could barely make out Kurt's shadowy, blurry silhouette as he prepared to hoist her up into his arms and out of harm's way. Surprising herself, she realized she actually welcomed the thought of his attentions. Kurt's hand broke through the surface into her world and she gladly reached out for him, a thrill shooting through her as he clasped her hand tightly.

She smiled up at him, realizing how seemingly compatible they were. She started to go over his good qualities in her head, when he asked, "See anything down there?" brought back to reality, she remembered why she was here in the first place. It was not the appropriate time or place for romance. Firmly, she tucked her brand new feelings away, knowing they would resurface again soon for there are simply some feelings you cannot deny forever.

CHAPTER TWENTY-EIGHT

Somewhere off the warm southern coastal waters of Florida, Drake Hanson and his granddaughter, Alisha, were shrimping from his boat, affectionately named the *Miss Priss*. Drake had been running shrimp boats for as long as he could remember, but had plans of retiring soon. He loved having Alisha in to visit from her home in South Charleston, West Virginia.

It was a yearly ritual for her to spend at least two weeks with her grandparents in Florida, but since her grandmother's death last year, this visit had been a tough one for the normally vibrant child. Drake had talked with his daughter Wendy, Alisha's mother, at length about maybe skipping this year because he felt it might be too soon after her grandmother's death. However, she begged to come, and he was hard pressed to deny her anything. She was the type of girl that never took no for an answer anyway. Drake was extremely pleased just the same that she still wanted to come. Alisha was his only grandchild and they had always had a great time together. He spoiled her rotten and she was his pride and joy.

Alisha was a spunky, fiercely independent eleven-year-old, and she held all the vitality of life in her fragile little hands. She loved all life's unexpected treasures and everyone who came in contact with her felt her warmth and charm. It made Drake feel young again having her around. He found himself constantly trying to look at the world through her innocent, untainted eyes. It was plain to see she was very special to her grandfather and the same held true for Alisha.

"Gramps!" Alisha hollered.

Drake stopped whistling the old show tune that was his go-to, and slowly rose up from the nets he had just pulled in. He turned, taking his Australian outback, khaki hat from his head and wiping the sweat from his brow using the sleeve of his shirt. Squinting, he looked into the sunlight at Alisha's profile. "Yes, babe?"

Alisha stood, smiling, her bibbed over-alls covered with fish guts and blood. Her long brown hair, tied in a ponytail, had worked its way out of the clasp from the ocean's strong breeze and was now whipping frantically back and forth in front of her face. She reminded Drake a lot of his daughter at that age.

"I'm really hungry. We should take a break soon, shouldn't we?" she said, looking to her grandfather and turning on her puppy dog charm.

"We sure should, honey. You're absolutely right! I think we're past due for one." Drake looked up at the sun and then to his watch, which read 12:45. He was so happy Alisha was with him that time just flew by. He had completely forgotten about lunch.

"I'll get lunch, Gramps!" Alisha excitedly shouted, as she scurried over to the cooler. She pulled out two frosty root beers and some peanut butter and mayo sandwiches, a weird combination as both of them shared the same eccentric appetite.

"Thanks, Lish," he smiled.

"You're welcome," she smiled back.

Drake frowned, realizing his little princess was somewhat reserved today. Thinking that she was probably thinking of her Granny, he felt incredibly helpless on how to console her. Granny had rarely gone shrimping with them. This was a special thing she only did with her Gramps.

"We're not doing too bad today, are we, honey? The weather's been pretty fair too," he said, trying to get her to open up to conversation.

"Yep, Gramps. I'm getting lots of sun. I think I'll put on some more sunscreen in a bit."

There was companionable silence again, each lost in their own thoughts as they ate their sandwiches, swigging tasty foaming root beer after each bite. The cool ocean breeze was a welcome relief from the hundred-degree heat. The boat swayed back and forth, promising to lull Drake to sleep as he leaned his tired body against the Miss Priss' interior wall, closing his eyes to rest.

There was nothing like being at one with the sea. It relaxed him, and he was at peace with the world. This boat had been his inner sanctum when his wife passed away. Countless hours were spent at sea, simply staring at the horizon. He loved the way the colors melted together into nothingness. It had been a major part of his personal healing process. He missed his wife dearly, but he was old enough to know that although they say time heals all wounds, it was not really true. His grief never went away; he just learned how to live with it, learned how to function again.

In the midst of his deep thoughts, he heard the wood from the crane that held the nets begin to slowly creak, louder and louder, under the weight of an unseen catch. Uneasiness crept slowly over every nerve in his body. Last time he heard that sound, a whale calf was caught in his nets.

"Gramps, what was that?" Alisha asked, startled by the sound.

Drake rose to his feet and smiled down at Alisha, "It's probably nothing. You go ahead and finish your sandwich. I'll take a look-see." He tousled her hair playfully as he walked away.

Drake had to think fast; he did not want Alisha to see a whale calf, or any other animal, struggling in the nets. She had such a soft heart for animals and he did not want to see it broken.

The creaking grew louder and more violent. He picked up his pace, all the while trying to be nonchalant so as not to alert Alisha to his worries. The pole that held the netting bounced up and down, like a cracking whip.

"What on earth?" Drake mumbled under his breath. He looked over the edge expecting to see a whale, but what he saw surprised him. There was absolutely nothing.

The net violently bobbed up and down where it entered the water. He turned and jetted to the crane controls. He did not want to chance stripping the gears, but he had no alternative course. Starting the motor, he firmly slipped it into low gear and tried slowly pulling the net in, but with no luck. He let out some drag and the net's tension only loosened a little before it tightened again.

"Gramps? What's going on?" Alisha asked, concern written all over her young face.

"Alisha dear, go back! I don't want you to get hurt. I'll be there in a minute."

Alisha could tell her Gramps was very serious. She was scared, but she did as she was told just the same.

Drake did not want to frighten her, but he had no choice. He had to deal with this situation first. He would take care of Alisha when things calmed down a bit. He was puzzled and his mind raced as he contemplated his next move. When he let out the slack, the net barely moved. Whatever was down there was not even trying to get away, but was munching on his harvest! The fact that something was stealing his livelihood and was at the same time throwing a monkey wrench in his time with Alisha angered him.

The only thing left to do would be to cut the nets, but that would be costly to him and the sea life. What else was he to do though? Whatever was down there could end up pulling the whole boat under. He had no other choice; he had to cut the net. It was just too risky to leave it to chance, especially since he had Alisha on board. Opening his tool chest, he pulled out a machete and hurriedly made his way back to the net. Out of the corner of his eye he noticed that Alisha looked very frightened, but he would have to tend to her later.

He reared back and swung the machete with all his might. Snapping sounds rippled through the air as the blade penetrated the tough netting that had bunched up and knotted at a point. He swung again, as his first blow did not completely sever the coarse netting. Again, the same results, but he did manage to cut a little deeper. With the third and final blow, the netting whipped by Drake, catching him sharply just below his right eye, inflicting several lacerations. Squealing, he grabbed the side of his face and fell to his knees as a burning sensation overcame him. In all the confusion, Alisha came to his aid.

"Gramps!" Alisha came to his aid, but one look at her face told Drake everything he needed to know; she was terrified. He pulled her to him and held onto her tightly. The boat still pitched and rocked like a carnival ride gone bad.

"What? It can't be still be doing this!" Drake broke away from Alisha and looked down over the railing. Searching everywhere, his eyes finally found what he was searching for. The net was caught on a rod located at the lower part of the boat. He knew what he had to do.

He glanced back at Alisha and tried to be as reassuring as he possibly could be, given their predicament. "Darling, everything will be alright." Her timid smile and the single nod of her head gave Drake courage. She believed in her Gramps, and he felt that in his soul.

Drake leaned precariously over the side of the boat and balanced himself against the Miss Priss' railing so as not to fall overboard when he swung his machete. He dangled more or less upside down just about a foot from the water. Maneuvering himself into place so as not to hit the boat with the machete, he flinched as the salt water burned his eyes and flesh wounds. Fresh blood dripped into the water below, instantly dissipating as he stretched as far as he could while swinging at the net, yet still only grazing it.

"Great googley moogley!" he shouted, frustrated, as he once again had to reposition himself. After a few moments spent maneuvering, he swung one more time.

"Yes!" he screamed, completely exhausted, as he watched the net disappear into the depths.

Within the split second it took to cut the net free, before he could even begin to pull himself up, a dark entity rose from the depths, where it had been waiting and watching, and seized the back of Drake's head. He automatically stiffened, and his legs instinctively tightened their grip on the railing, holding on for dear life. But the grip on his head was much too strong, and his shock turned to utter fear when he realized his head was in the jaws of a shark. Drake did not have the strength to fight it, and zero amount of adrenaline came to his aid. The predator effortlessly snatched him from his boat, where he would never again see the horizon, the sea, or worse than anything, his Lisha.

Alisha's blood-curdling screams filled the air as the black terror claimed its kill. The waters rose and sank with savagery as Drake's body was maliciously devoured. With the splintering of his bones and laceration of his sinews, the feast had begun. In a matter of moments, Drake joined his wife in the heavens.

Alisha stood rooted at the edge of the boat where her Gramps had once been, staring horrified into the unforgiving ocean below. Tears from her cheeks fell like raindrops into the bloodstained water that had swallowed up the man she had loved more than anything.

She slowly backed a step away as a single partially submerged, jagged fin hovered in place, as if to taunt her and show dominance over its prize. Under the surface of the water, Alisha met cold dark eyes, their menacing stare burning a hole into her heart before the beast placidly turned, disappearing into the underworld below.

CHAPTER TWENTY-NINE

Amanda sat quietly on the edge of the deck, staring intently into the blue waters. She had changed out of her scuba gear and was trying desperately to make sense of it all. Kurt had gone below several minutes ago, giving her the opportunity to simply sit and run things through her head. She was confused, but her head was awash with several possible explanations for the Malangus' loss of power.

Kurt's eyes adjusted to the darkness of the lavatory as he closed the door and did his business. He leaned his head back and closed his eyes, as he began rotating his head in a clockwise direction, stretching the now sore, stress-filled muscles in his neck. It felt good to relax for a moment. Suddenly, like magic, light filled the bathroom, startling Kurt as he momentarily strained his vision. He quickly grabbed the bathroom door handle and busted into the noisy control room where everything that had been dead and silent came unexpectedly back to life.

Amanda was already scampering down the stairs as Kurt looked around.

"We've got power!" Kurt said joyfully, like a kid who just got exactly what he wanted for Christmas. Kurt walked over to join Amanda and they both looked to the sonar—nothing—then to the underwater camera monitor—nothing. Amanda tried panning in and out on the underwater cameras that encompassed the Malangus, but sadly they still saw nothing.

Kurt pressed down the radio toggle switch and leaned into the mike, as he said, "This is Dr. Wyatt of the Malangus. Can anyone read me?"

There was a brief silence.

"Dr. Wyatt, it's good to hear from you. This is Captain Lucas. Is everything alright?"

Amanda and Kurt sighed simultaneously in relief.

"Everything's all clear here, Captain!" Kurt said. "I don't know what happened, but our equipment went berserk and we lost all power. Coincidentally, we lost the sharks at about the same time... or should I say, the sharks lost us?"

Kurt frowned and looked at the ceiling, puzzled at the loud noise that could suddenly be heard just above the Malangus.

"I'll check it out," Amanda whispered to Kurt, and he nodded in agreement. She dashed up the stairs and Kurt couldn't help but notice the way she confidently flounced her hair as she turned to go. He chuckled as he realized what a ridiculous time it had been to notice this small detail about her.

"I've just been notified that one of our copters has located your ship. Do you need assistance?"

The voice crackling over the radio jolted him out of his brief distraction. "I'm not sure. Our power had just come back on right before I contacted you. I still need to see if this baby will turn over."

"We are approximately two miles due south. We'll be there soon, so just stay put till we get there. There are some things I need to discuss with you and Dr. Paige."

"Sure; we'll be waiting for you," Kurt responded, turning as Amanda reentered the room.

"It's a Coast Guard heli, and a ship is also approaching in the distance," Amanda announced, a grin firmly in place.

CHAPTER THIRTY

It was probably the longest day Kurt could ever remember, or wanted to remember for that matter. The meeting with Admiral Edwards, of the Coast Guard, and Admiral Wildey, of the Navy, produced no startling revelations. They were able to view the gruesome massacre footage compliments of ESPN 2, which covered the dreadful event, but there was still much more to be learned. The sharks were now nowhere to be found, having disappeared as quickly as they had appeared. The ocean was a vast place, making it very difficult to locate anything, especially sea life. Still, the Coast Guard and the Navy were making every effort to find the sharks and, hopefully, prevent anyone from entering the waters and falling victim to their ravenous appetite. All expectations were placed upon Amanda and Kurt for answers, but the very simple fact of the matter was they needed much more to go on.

Amanda and Kurt arrived back at the MOL at about 5:00 p.m. They opened the door to find Shane bent over a microscope tediously taking notes. He had a pencil, sharpened all the way down to the eraser, in one hand and a slice of veggie pizza, half of which Amanda was certain had been inadvertently spilled on his shirt, in the other. They stood at the door, silently laughing at him while his head bounced up and down in time to the heavy metal that blared from the stereo.

Shane glanced up and jumped quickly in surprise as he reached to turn the volume on the stereo down, leaving a rather large piece of mushroom and some red sauce behind on the knob.

"Dr. Wyatt, Dr. Paige, good to see you. I prepared the specimens like you requested and I think you'll find this one especially interesting," Shane jumped up and said, his mouth half full of pizza.

Kurt had radioed Shane from the Malangus once he regained radio power and asked him to prepare specimens from the fatalities at the tournament, interview the survivors, and take photos of the survivors' wounds. Kurt was very proud of his assistant. Shane reminded him much of himself at that age: slightly disorganized but intelligent, hard-working, full of energy and determination, and eager to tackle any obstacle that was put before him. He could not have asked for a better assistant, possessing all of those qualities and more.

Shane paused for a moment and shook his head. "Where are my manners? Have some pizza and iced tea. I knew y'all would probably be starving so I ordered out."

"Thanks," Kurt obliged and grabbed a slice as Amanda looked into the microscope's eyepiece. She continued staring for some time while the other two waited for her reaction. Kurt picked up the pictures Shane had taken of the wounded, pieces of body parts and flesh, and was studying them carefully.

"It's a good thing this is a veggie pizza!" Kurt remarked, shaking his head in disbelief as he viewed the hideous photographs.

"Shane, what do you make of it?" Kurt asked, not looking up, but continuing to examine the pictures.

"Well, from the accounts from the wounded survivors, as well as the body parts and tissue we recovered, they all show the same bite patterns as the Orcas and jet ski did. Of those I interviewed, the recurring themes were that they just appeared... like from out of nowhere; that it seemed like they were everywhere they turned; that they worked like a well-trained team, as though each knew exactly what the other was thinking; and that there was no escape."

He continued, "Witnesses reported they saw what seemed to be a huge dark mass moving through the clear waters towards their victims. They said all you could see was hundreds of weird looking jagged fins moving at an unimaginable pace. They were attacking before anyone realized what was going on, and by then it was too late. Mass hysteria ensued, of course, with the sharks thrashing, and people struggling and screaming as the blue waters turned to crimson. People on the beach did as much as they could, but it was over in a matter of minutes, and when the smoke cleared the sharks had vanished."

Shane paused momentarily as he shifted through his notes. "Oh yes, the major descriptions given were limited to their color, which was totally black, however, interestingly enough, not *just* black, but almost *too* black, and their distinctively jagged fins, which were particularly mesmerizing. Their sizes seemed to range from five to eight feet in length." Shane looked up from his notes to Dr. Wyatt, making sure he was following.

"Please continue," Kurt said, gulping down another swig of tea and examining the test results Shane had brought back from the university.

"Sure. As you know, approximately fifty-four victims have been claimed by these sharks to date. That number, in my opinion, is certainly guaranteed to continue to rise as missing persons reports flood the local law enforcement agencies in the surrounding areas."

"And that's actually not even counting the missing persons reports made before the tournament," Kurt added. "I watched these sharks as they pursued us for miles. I must have counted one hundred plus. I know it's terrible what they are doing, but I wish you could have seen them, Shane. If you could have only seen how absolutely breathtaking they were. I've never seen anything so horribly beautiful in my entire life." Kurt hovered behind Amanda in anticipation for his turn at the microscope.

Amanda studied the last slide and rose up, shaking her head in amazement. "Is this really true? It's astonishing!"

"I thought the same, but the evidence doesn't lie," Shane said, nudging Kurt closer to the microscope.

Kurt didn't say a word, but moved in front of Amanda to take a look for himself. The room fell silent as Kurt did a double take. "This just can't be possible." Kurt continued to examine the slides.

Amanda broke in, "I think I can make the assumption by the broken tooth fragment lodged in this human tissue, along with the bite patterns from the other specimens, that this is presumably an entirely new species of shark. The patterns are extremely uneven, which tells me the individual teeth are abnormally lined in the jawbone."

"I agree, the teeth have to be exceedingly uneven and irregular, leading me to believe they are jagged serrated teeth that are malformed or deformed in the jaw. You got a glimpse of them while they were chasing us, right?" Kurt's eyes met Amanda's. "Those wicked fins and the solid black color even appeared on their undersides."

"Well, we've said there's much to be learned about the undiscovered seas, but this is ludicrous. Where have they been hiding?" Shane asked, flabbergasted.

"That's what we need to find out," Amanda looked at them sternly.

All three of them were curious about this new find. They were concerned for the safety of mankind, of course, but as marine biologists, this was what they had waited for all their lives. There would be much sleep lost and tons of work ahead of them, but they welcomed it with opened arms. A sharp knock came from the door and they all jerked simultaneously as they were startled out of their deep thoughts.

"I'll get it," Shane offered. Opening the door, Shane saw the silhouettes of two uniformed men standing in the darkness of the night.

"I am Admiral Edwards, and this is Vice Admiral Ruby. We're with the U.S. Coast Guard. We would like to speak with Dr. Wyatt and Dr. Paige, please."

"Sure, they're inside." Shane squinted into the dark to view the visitors. "Please, come right in," Shane said, finally stepping aside to allow them inside.

CHAPTER THIRTY-ONE

Amanda and Kurt jointly decided to venture out bright and early in the morning to search for the elusive new species. The tattered remains of night fought defiantly against the dawn, and a sticky, dense fog hung in the air making it extremely difficult to see the oncoming waters. The Malangus glided smoothly through the Atlantic toward the site where they had last seen the sharks the day before. Both scientists were visibly anxious and tried to mask their anticipation through idle chat. A couple of hours passed in what seemed like minutes as the sun slowly won its battle with the foggy darkness.

Amanda's exhaustion from the day before had miraculously departed overnight. She now felt fully restored and invigorated. It did not quite make sense though, because she was under a great deal of stress and sleep had not come easily. Why complain for feeling good though, she thought.

Kurt gradually put the Malangus into low gear before shutting off the engine. The abrupt absence of the constant humming of the engine created a barren silence. Nothing but the sound of the waves gently licking at the hull could be heard. Amanda looked coyly up into the cockpit, excited to see Kurt smiling devilishly down at her. She rubbed her arms as the little hairs prickled with excitement. The tension between the two was easily tangible. She thought that Kurt was as interested in her as she was in him and she wanted nothing more than for him to put it out there, make it known. She longed to really get to know him in a more intimate way. Was he sweet? Protective? Loyal? Would he hold her tenderly when she'd had a rough day?

Am I going to have to make the first move? If this goes on much longer, I might have to, she thought.

"Well, this is it. We're here!" Kurt announced, descending the ladder fireman-style, sliding with both feet on the outside of the rails. Amanda was both surprised and impressed at his agility; he was a scientist, after all, not a stuntman. She was sure he intentionally brushed against her on his way to lower the anchor. Amanda caught her breath as she felt Kurt's warmth as he passed by. She could not wait any longer, her newfound feelings suddenly over-riding her normal sense of demure propriety. She pursued him down the side of the boat, careful not to appear as though she was chasing after him.

Kurt stopped and stood before the anchor's controls and let the anchor down. It made a *kerplunk* sound as it hit the water's surface and plummeted towards the depths.

Amanda stood behind him, waiting for the opportunity to make her move. She had never done this before; men had always approached her first. She suddenly realized how intimidating it was and she mentally gave credit to every guy that had ever had the nerve to ask her out. Kurt's back was still to her as she pondered her options.

She was nervous, for sure. This was not her style at all, but she decided to rely on her gut instincts and do what came naturally.

She was shivering from nervousness and her mouth felt like she had swallowed a box of cotton balls, but she was dead set on doing this. She took a few steps towards him, making it nearly impossible for Kurt to get away; he was pinned. Her fingers fidgeted together as she tried to figure out the right words to say, words that made a statement without making her sound like a tart. She backed up a step, deciding maybe it was not the right time yet, knowing it was really just cowardice that made that decision for her.

Unexpectedly, he turned, startled at her nearness. "Oh, hello," Kurt murmured softly. Instead of quickly skirting around her as she had expected, he stood there grinning. His deep blue eyes captivated her, rooting her in place. Even when he reached up to gently tuck her windblown hair behind her ear, she could not have moved even if she had wanted to.

"Have I mentioned today how beautiful you are?"

Shaking her head, her wide eyes searched his face for some resolution of truth. Was he joking with her? If so, it came at a most vulnerable time for her. She had not even noticed a man since her break-up, but here she was, suddenly developing a quite a fondness for Dr. Kurt Wyatt. And why not? He was good looking—a catch by anyone's standards. Yet there she stood, tongue-tied, like a silly schoolgirl eyeing the captain of the football team for the first time.

She sighed and dropped her head, shifting her eyes away from his, feeling the stain of embarrassment flood her cheeks. She had obviously not thought this through enough. Even though she knew everything worth knowing about sea-life, sharks in particular, and even though most people would rightly class her as a genius, she could not even string a simple sentence together to tell this man in front of her that she was interested in him.

As she started to turn away from him, he surprised her by taking her hand in his and pulling her closer. "I mean it, Amanda. From the first moment I saw you until now, you've been on my mind. You're the most beautiful woman I've ever seen."

Amanda shivered slightly, whether from the slight chill in the air or from Kurt's fingertips tracing up her arms leaving goose bumps in their wake, she did not know.

As his fingers found their final destination, cradling her face just below her chin, she wondered if he could sense the wild beating of her heart. Kurt pulled her closer, timidly brushing his lips against hers.

His hands came back to rest on her waist and he effortlessly hoisted her up onto the deck banister of the ship. Nothing in the world mattered at this point—not her work, her life, or the sharks— she was happy, and she was going to enjoy every moment of it. She felt warm and safe... and in love.

Kurt smiled at her, again brushing the wind blown hair away from her beaming face. "Do you think you could perhaps we could…"

Thud! Thud! Thud!

Something smashed into the boat, impacting it enough to knock Amanda off balance just as Kurt lost his grip on her. She fell from the boat and there was nothing either one of them could do about it. Falling helplessly backwards into the water below, she could see Kurt's terrified face as he grabbed for her in vain.

Time magically slowed, and she felt as though she was falling in slow motion. She had enough time to see the vile fate that awaited her. They somehow knew she would fall, and the predators were right there waiting for her when she did.

The evil black creatures were writhing on top of one another, some of them literally out of the water, waiting anxiously for the opportunity to thrash Amanda's body to pieces. She screamed, realizing her fate. With a final agonizing look toward Kurt, she held her breath and awaited her watery grave.

Amanda jerked awake, wide-eyed in the darkness, breathing at an unearthly rate with her heart was pounding out of her ribcage. She stared into nothingness as she lay in her sweat-drenched bed, staring up at the darkness of the MOL's ceiling. Confused and disoriented for a moment, she finally came to the realization it had all been a dream—a beautiful and terrifying dream.

She gazed at the clock beside her foldaway bed, which displayed half past four. The MOL stood silently as Kurt and Shane slept quietly in the next room. Had she screamed out, or said anything she would be embarrassed about later? She listened intently, grateful that only silence prevailed.

Relieved they had not heard her scream, she fell back onto her pillow and attempted to go back to sleep. Slumber evaded her, however, and she tossed and turned, her mind churning with no apparent off switch. All she could think about was the dream before the sharks had come along. She tried to remember as much about it as she could, closing her eyes and picturing Kurt and her together. It had been sweet and romantic, and it left her wondering whether pursuing more than just sharks on this expedition was something she should consider. She had been furtively watching him over the past several days and knew that he was a kind and considerate man with too many good qualities to name. The more time she spent with him, the more she realized he was exactly the kind of man she thought no longer existed—a good man, plain and simple.

Her eyes grew heavy once more and she was drifting toward sleep when the part of her dream that she consistently pushed away entered her conscience again—the shark attack. Her eyes popped wide open again. Why had such a beautiful dream been marred by such a horrifying and tragic ending? Was it nothing but a mere dream—a story simply merging the two entities that had taken up most of her time recently? Or was it her subconscious warning her that a relationship right now was a dangerous move?

CHAPTER THIRTY-TWO

At a secluded area just north of Turtle Beach, an illegal drift net operation was hastily underway in the dark recesses of the night. The boat's crewmembers, which had laid several nets earlier, were now gathering up the remaining nets. They had been strategically placed, as they were almost every night. Even though driftnet fishing had been outlawed in U.S. waters, this, like many other things that were illegal, was an easy moneymaker. Gilbert Blanche, otherwise known as Gib, and his rough-cut crewmen had the illicit practice down to a science. They had everything covered, according to what was known as *Gib's Rules*. They were a fairly simple set of guidelines established by the boss, designed specifically for his line of work - the vigilant monitoring of radio frequencies, never fishing in the same location twice in one week, easy access to bailing out if need be, and the covering of their tracks.

Gib stared at his glowing watch. Releasing the light button, he hissed at his crew. "We're running behind! Let's pick it up, ladies!"

There were two remaining nets to retrieve, but so far they had not caught much of anything. Gib watched in silent frustration as net after net yielded little. It came like anything else in life—you took the bad with the good. He hoped the bad would turn to good with the two remaining nets. The men had just finished hooking up the next to the last net and were preparing to bring it aboard.

"Let's do this," Gib ordered the man at the controls. The pulley started its familiar creaking clamor as the tension created by the driftnets was levied on the crank. Gib could already calculate by the small amount of strain placed on the motor this catch was going to be minuscule. A stream light was directed into the murky waters below, providing ample light to see the unfortunate creatures that had met their end.

Gib took a rumpled pack of gum from his vest pocket. Roughly pulling the last stick from its torn end, he winced as he opened his mouth, feeling the stinging burn. His lips were so chapped he knew he would have a few new splits in the rough skin before morning.

"Well, that just makes my day," he uttered sarcastically as he headed towards the bow of the boat.

"Gib! Get over here quick and check this out!" yelled one of the burly crewmen.

Gib immediately halted in his tracks and started back to the driftnets, all the while scanning for uninvited guests, a.k.a. the authorities. Thanks to his strict rules, he had only one close call in all his years, and he hoped not to have another.

"What's up?" Gib asked, tossing the crumpled gum wrapper into the water. When he saw the net was completely tangled and shredded to bits, he already had his answer.

"Geez! What on earth happened here?" Gib blew up, looking over the netting hoping for some clue to its destruction. The men around him also stared at the netting in confusion, awaiting some direction from him.

"Mr. Blanche, do you want us to cut it free? The net is useless to us now anyway," said a young worker who had only been with Gib for a couple of weeks. The others turned their backs, knowing what was coming and grimacing in preparation.

"No, we're not going to cut it free! And do you know why we're not going to cut it free, son?" Gib asked, sarcasm dripping from his voice like molasses.

The young man paused for a moment with his head down, like a school kid who had just been chastised by the principal. "Because of the other sea-life and the environment?" he ventured in a shameful and barely audible reply.

Rubbing the back of his neck and shaking his head in frustration, Gib replied harshly, "No, son, I couldn't care less what a bunch of tree huggers think of me! Let me make it simple for ya! If the net shows up out of nowhere, then law enforcement starts looking for answers, and we don't need the heat breathing down our backs. Gib's rules! Never leave any evidence!" He pointedly turned his back, looking again over the destroyed net and motioning absentmindedly for the man at the controls to continue.

Little by little, the net was brought up. Little by little, Gib grew more furious. His face turned a reddish blue hue and looked like it would pop at any moment. They could finally see the end of the net when one of his men hollered, "I think I see something big caught in the net."

"What is that thing?"

"I can't see it. What is it?"

"It's big, whatever it is."

The net was so wrapped up and tangled, it was difficult to make out exactly what was camouflaged as it was beneath the layers.

Gib snarled, bewildered, "Is it a dolphin or shark?"

"Ya got me," one of his men answered, shrugging his shoulders.

The unidentified creature was hoisted up onto the deck and the men gathered around, carefully cutting away the tangled netting.

It was shaped like a shark or a dolphin, but it was solid black. As each layer of netting was cut away, distinguishing features emerged until all the netting had been completely stripped away, but it never moved. They all stood there, bewildered and speechless.

"Sweet mother, what is that?" The closest man questioned, hesitantly. One by one, the others regained their ability to speak and murmured amongst themselves quietly.

Gib had never seen anything quite like this before. It was utterly repulsive. He was sure it was some kind of shark, but not like any shark he had ever seen before. It was approximately six feet long and the darkest black he had ever seen. He felt as if it was a void, sucking all the light right out of the air and simply crushing it into darkness. Even its cold, dead eyes reflected no light at all. The word *gruesome* came to mind as he noticed the jagged teeth, extruding from the jaw and jutting haphazardly in every direction.

Gib shuddered involuntarily as he closely scrutinized the otherworldly fish. The fin was the most perplexing, looking like someone had fashioned it with a jig saw. Even dead, the thing gave him the willies.

While Gib nor any of the others were scientists or oceanographers, they came to the almost certain conclusion that the unfortunate beast was just a shark—an unusual freak of nature, perhaps, but just a shark all the same.

"Throw it back in and let's get the last net in. We're gonna call it a night," Gib gruffly ordered.

Out of curiosity, the new worker reached down to touch the head of the shark before anyone could stop him.

"Don't even think about it, kid!" Gib shouted, lending his voice to the cacophony of the others shouting the same words.

Within a split second the shark came to life. Twisting its powerful body, the shark seized the man's hand and started biting its way up his arm in a mechanical chomping fashion. It feasted its way up his shoulder, the man screaming in agony and hopelessly attempting to pull away. The shark effortlessly whipped him about the deck. The men, using spears, shovels, and anything else they could readily find, began to beat or stab the creature. They did all they could, but the invincible shark instinctively ate flesh and crunched bones, never giving the desperate young lad any hope for escape.

Shots suddenly rang out from Gib's *Glock*. His bullets found their mark in the shark's head, quickly extinguishing every last bit of life from it. It was too late for the unfortunate soul lying motionless in a thick pool of blood. The shark, even in death, still had a firm grip on the man. The other men were horrified at the sight of their co-worker's dead eyes as they stared blankly from his half-eaten face. His life had been taken in a matter of seconds; the crew had been able to do nothing to save him. Now, they stood around the man in silent disbelief, words escaping them.

Gib's harsh voice broke the eerie silence. "What're you all looking at? Get that thing off him and let's get outta here," he shouted, angrily.

CHAPTER THIRTY-THREE

Abruptly awakened from the upsetting dream, Amanda tossed and turned for a bit, unable to find sleep again. It was hot in the small cabin. The longer she lay there trying to sleep, the hotter she felt. Finally, wiping beads of perspiration from her brow, she decided she might as well get up and work.

In the kitchen area, she made some hazelnut coffee, and sat at the table appreciating the sweet aroma that permeated the air. She did not sit there long, however; now that she was up and moving around, she felt the familiar pull to analyze the new specimens. Quickly gulping down the coffee she poured, still hot from the pot, she burned the inside of her mouth as a reward. So much was her excitement to begin working though, she barely noticed the pain as she opened the cooler to find what she wanted. Pulling out several of the bits and pieces, she carried them to the worktable in the center of the room and set up the tools she needed to make molds of them.

The couple of hours she had slept did her some good, but her passion for sharks fueled her energy level even more. She was determined to get to the bottom of this scientific mystery, even if it killed her. After a couple hours of work, as she waited for the molds to set, she reached for the coffee pot and poured herself another cup of the now syrupy brew. The phone rang abruptly, startling her and causing her to jerk, pouring coffee over the side of the cup burning her fingers.

"Yeoowww!" She cringed in pain as she placed the pot on the counter and raced for the phone, shaking her hand in the air and blowing wildly on her fingers hoping the pain would subside.

"Hello," she whispered, hoping not to wake Kurt or Shane. "Yes, Admiral Edwards, this is Dr. Paige."

Listening intently, she noticed that Shane, and then Kurt entered the room, both wiping sleep from their squinting eyes as they stretched and yawned. Both had inquiring but worried looks on their faces as they listened anxiously to Amanda's every word.

"That's horrible," she frowned, continuing to listen. Amanda turned her back on the guy's frowning faces, giving her full attention to Admiral Edwards. Kurt, refusing to be left out of the loop, childishly pressed his ear against the receiver of the phone beside Amanda's face in a feeble attempt to garner information. It was impossible for Amanda not to notice Kurt's lips, precariously close to hers, but she had to focus instead on the Admiral's words.

"Yes Admiral, we'll be right there," she pulled away from Kurt, glaring at him as she replied. "I understand. Thank you… yes… good-bye."

Amanda hung up the phone and looked at the two men, her face showing serious concern.

"That was Admiral Edwards. The Coast Guard has located a ship drifting with no signs of life aboard. They boarded the vessel and made a frightening discovery." She paused, taking first a deep breath and then a hard swallow. "Guys, this could be the break we've been waiting for. They found one of our sharks aboard—dead."

"What happened?" Shane eagerly asked.

"Well, it is apparently an illegal driftnet fisherman's boat. I can't really speculate what exactly happened, but I can guarantee they caught more than they bargained for. It gets worse than that," her voice grew painfully grim. "They found a dead man on board, still locked in the jaws of our shark."

The two men were motionless for a moment, but she could sense the barrage of questions building in their minds.

Amanda cut them off quick, "I don't know the whole story, but I'll fill you in on everything I do know on the way over to Cathelley Naval Base. The Coast Guard is towing this ship there now, so we can take a look. The Coast Guard and the Navy will be wanting solid answers fast, and they are looking to us for them."

They went their separate ways in the MOL, each getting ready and gathering the necessary equipment and supplies. They finished up and left the MOL in less than twenty minutes, which would put them at Cathelley a little before the estimated time of arrival of the mystery ship, which held their precious cargo.

*   *   *

When the U.S.C.G. Ashley arrived with the ship in tow, Amanda, Kurt, and Shane immediately boarded it, along with the other uniformed officers from the Coast Guard and Navy. The smell of rotting flesh, dead fish, and other marine creatures hung in the air like a wet blanket. The stench grew almost unbearable as they neared a tarpaulin covering the executioner and its victim. Amanda found herself instinctively covering her mouth and nose in an attempt to shelter her senses from the nauseating stench.

They met Captain Sader of the U.S.C.G. Ashley, whose crew had investigated this case. He saluted his superior officers and gave them the run down on what had been discovered.

"Thank you, Captain Sader. Job well done," Admiral Edwards praised. "Doctors, I think this is where you take over."

"Sure," Amanda said, as Kurt and Shane shook their heads in agreement.

Admiral Edwards subtly motioned to one of his officers to remove the tarp. All eyes were drawn to the appalling scene, as bit by bit the brutal act of savagery was unraveled. The foul odor was atrocious; even though they wore surgical masks, it was still intolerable. Kurt felt his knees buckle, but he caught himself and fought off the dizzy sensation that threatened to possess his body.

The shark had been ghastly enough in their imaginations, but seeing the way it really looked was even more terrifying. A couple of the officers turned their eyes away, while one ran to the edge of the boat and lost his last meal. It was not a pretty sight. There, lay a man with his entire right arm, shoulder, all the way into his face consumed by this shark. The poor man's barely recognizable, half-eaten face told the terror he had lived through the last few seconds of his life. His one remaining eye was still wide open in horror, and his mouth was now permanently frozen in death as it echoed his silent screams of agony.

Words could not come close to describing how utterly repulsive and evil the shark appeared to be. Its bullet-riddled body had finally met its match, but not before claiming yet another unsuspecting victim.

Even in death, the shark seems to be gloating over its prize, thought Kurt.

A surreal gloom surrounded the grisly scene as, one by one, Kurt, Amanda, and Shane slowly turned their heads and walked a few steps away in an attempt to distance themselves from the atrocity.

CHAPTER THIRTY-FOUR

It was no easy chore prying the shark away from the unlucky gentleman. The officers had to resort to breaking some of the shark's teeth off, but eventually they managed to separate the unholy unification. The man, whose identity was unknown, was eventually taken to the county Medical Examiner's office for a thorough examination, while the shark was taken to the naval laboratory facility on base.

Amanda and Kurt took a copious amount of notes and collected as much data as they could. Shane, a little too eagerly, took both pictures and videos of the shark and the unfortunate man. The scene investigation took a little over three hours and the Coast Guard and Navy still had their own investigations to perform.

Shane gathered up all the notes as Kurt gave him a message to pass along to president of the university. "Oh yeah, tell President Caterine I'll try to call him a little later. Thanks."

"Sure thing," Shane said as he left for the university to pick up some necessary items and test results.

At the Navy's warehouse bay where the shark was soon to arrive, Amanda had been on the phone inside the small warehouse office for some time talking to her office in Australia.

Amanda and Kurt had previously discussed the thought of asking other professionals for their opinions or knowledge of the subject, but the more they talked it over, the more it seemed pointless. They were the leading experts on sharks in the world, and due to the circumstances, there was not enough time to bring in other people.

Amanda wrapped up her phone call as Kurt entered the warehouse. To him, her conversation sounded like a foreign language as everything that was said echoed throughout the empty building and bounced off the walls. She turned as he entered the office, and smiled in his direction, holding his gaze as she realized they would be forever linked together for this scientific find. He warmly smiled back, returning the look she gave him intently. He was happy he'd had the forethought to call her in on this project at the very beginning, but even more than her expertise, Kurt was excited for the time he would get to spend with her. His marriage to Miranda had been exceptionally happy. Never in a million years did he think he would find another woman with whom he might be happy—until now.

Amanda looked away briefly to hang up the phone, and then slowly turned back to find Kurt's eyes still locked on her. Her face flushed as the overwhelming emotions she'd made herself bury the night before surfaced once again.

The brief moment ended all too soon when the giant metal doors of the warehouse screeched loudly as they opened, and a covered flatbed truck noisily roared its way inside.

Kurt regretfully pried his eyes from Amanda's to watch the truck enter the building. The fumes and the heat from outside filled the air-conditioned facility. He welcomed the warmth. He loved the outdoors and the feel of the sun on his back. Several officers surrounded the truck, while another drove a forklift over and picked up the pallet upon which the covered shark lay. They walked behind the forklift as it drove its cargo into a giant walkin cooler. Admiral Wildey entered the warehouse through a door beside the cooler and motioned for Amanda and Kurt to follow him.

They entered a large, state-of-the-art laboratory with a giant Plexiglas window lining one wall. From there, they could observe the activity within the cooler. They watched as the forklift backed out of the cooler after dropping its load, the large doors closed boldly.

"I hope you find this to your liking," the Admiral boasted.

Amanda's eyes wandered throughout the lab in amazement. "This sure is a nice lab you have here. I'm impressed you have such a state-of-the art facility at your disposal," Amanda said, flattering the Admiral immensely.

"Well, we have to be prepared for anything. If there is something you need—anything—just ask one of my officers and they will assist you," the Admiral directed toward Amanda.

"Thank you, Admiral," Kurt cut in. "Would it be possible for us to move my Mobile Oceanographic Laboratory inside this warehouse? Your laboratory is well equipped, but there are additional items we'll need. It will also give us a break from the inevitable reporters."

"Sure, Dr. Wyatt. Whatever you need; we aim to please," the Admiral replied, his smile not quite reaching his eyes. "As you learn more about those monsters, please let me know immediately. The President is at the end of his rope, and I need some answers quick." Hesitating for a moment, he continued. "Excuse my impatience, ma'am," he said pleasantly in Amanda's direction, tilting his hat forward in a graceful manner. "I'm sure you'll agree that time is of the essence here."

"Yes sir, we know. We are working as fast as we can. We want to get to the bottom of this just as much as you do," Amanda agreed, her voice firm and her eyes steely.

The Admiral hesitated, then nodded his head curtly and closed the door behind him, leaving Amanda and Kurt alone.

"What's the matter with him? Doesn't he know we're doing all we can?" Amanda questioned.

"He knows we are," Kurt smiled, realizing that Amanda had no clue she had just shot down a four-star admiral. "That's just the military way. And this is a very stressful situation. Don't take it personally."

"You're right," she smiled, starting to relax again. "Let's take a closer look at our shark, shall we?"

CHAPTER THIRTY-FIVE

The sun's rays weighed heavily on the weary crusaders within the small handmade boat made of scrap wood, fiberglass, and other odd and ends. No one could open their eyes completely as the blinding light and sweat had already taken a toll on their vision. Ricardo had constructed his *Ship to Freedom* in secrecy over a period of several months, with the assistance of his younger brother, Berto, in Cuba. He dared not work on it during the day for fear of government retaliation. He knew that some day he would take his family and seek independence in America.

Now was that time, for he, his wife Reesa, his son Rico age five, and baby daughter of eleven months, Donea, were on that momentous voyage, hoping to make themselves a better life. Like so many others who had gone before him, he was well aware of the danger involved, but he was still willing to risk everything for freedom—and so, by night they had boarded the makeshift boat, said a prayer, and placed themselves at the mercy of the sea and God.

Three excruciating days had come and gone, and they would be lucky if their meager food and water supplies would last them a couple more. Ricardo had tried to make a canvas umbrella-type apparatus to shield them from the sun's burning rays. He felt such guilt for the pain of his children. Lips parched and cracked, they still managed a smile when he winked playfully at them. He was trying to keep the family's spirits up, but it was becoming increasingly difficult. There had been no rain the entire trip, and he did not know whether to wish for it or not, because rain would mean the possibility of treacherous storms.

By night, Ricardo would slowly row his crude self-designed craft in the direction of the United States. He navigated by reading the stars, a skill he had learned from old-time mariners on the island. His torn up hands were badly swollen. They had been blistered to the point where bandages were a necessity to keep the flesh from being scraped away from his palms, but still, he would not dare stop rowing.

By day, they slept, huddled under the umbrella, resting for the demanding night ahead of them. Ricardo had heard the tales of others being caught by the authorities or being lost at sea, never to be found or heard from again. He knew it was a dangerous endeavor, but it had become so bad he felt it justified and worth the risk for the safety and well-being of his family.

They slept fitfully in the inescapable heat of the sun, the boat lazily lulling back and forth, a motion they had gradually grown accustomed to. Ricardo was just about to nod off into a light sleep when he was jolted awake by something nudging the boat, but he had been half asleep.

Had it only been his imagination?

Ricardo stared at the canvas over his head, watching its tattered, threadbare fringes flap in the wind, waiting for something to either happen or not happen; the latter being the one he preferred. His temples pounded in expectation, as the fear built inside him that something was terribly wrong. The hair on the back of his neck stood at attention, separating themselves from his sweat-soaked body. His senses peaked, but all that could be heard were the waves gently lapping against the boat and the fluttering from the canvas above.

He looked to his family, still sleeping with not a care in the world. Finally relaxing and settling himself to get some much-needed sleep, something in his brain impelled him he'd better take a look, just to be on the safe side.

Ricardo pulled his weary body up just enough to observe the surrounding waters. He tried to swallow, but a lump the size of his fist had formed suddenly in his throat as his mind unsuccessfully attempted to grasp the full reality of what he saw. Shark fins completely encircled the boat! Ricardo's mind overloaded with panicked thoughts. Should he wake his family? No, he decided. He did not want to alarm them for fear they might excite the sharks to attack. Taking several deep breaths, he nervously pondered his next move. He could see the shapes of darkness gliding about the waters, sinister dorsal fins occasionally protruding as if taunting him of the eminent danger. He was too frightened to do anything, but sweat it out, praying silently they would leave him and his family alone.

Again, another nudge, but this one more forceful than the last. Ricardo clutched the sides of the boat, shifting his weight to counteract the hits and balance the vessel, so as not to wake his family. Holding his breath as Donea rustled a bit, he softly exhaled again as she snuggled quietly back to sleep against her mother's breast.

Angrily, Ricardo struggled to make a decision of what he should do. He had no alternatives, but to remain silent and hope the predators would just go away.

What else can I do? his thoughts raced aimlessly. Fearfully, he slowly rose to again survey the area encompassing the boat.

Shock was now his only companion—not only were the sharks still present, but they were multiplying in numbers! A dark cloud of terror surrounded the boat, dismissive of the glare from the sun. Ricardo's clothes were drenched with perspiration and the sweat from his forehead stung his eyes. Oxygen seemed to leave his body faster than he could gasp for air. He could only imagine that the end was near. Of course, he feared for his own life, but much worse, he feared for his family. All his adult life, he had tried to make a better life for them. They were his sole purpose for living; he would have done anything for them, but now he realized what his actions had caused. He wept silently, roughly brushing his tears away. Repeatedly reciting prayer, he clutched the silver crucifix he had worn about his neck since childhood.

The strikes to the boat became more numerous, more severe. Had they only been testing him before? He knew he had to do something; he was running out of time. Carefully bringing himself to his knees and maintaining balance, he reached for the one of the oars. Maybe he could just row his way out of this horror.

Ricardo placed one oar into the water, but it was instantly snatched from his hand. "Auuugghhh!" Ricardo moaned in pain as he pulled his bloodied hands back to his sides. Stiffening in fear as his family began to stir, a decision was swiftly made. He jerked the other oar up from the boat and quickly dug it into the water, beginning to row at a frantic pace.

"Papa?" Rico murmured sleepily, roused by the commotion.

Ricardo's vacant eyes fixed painfully on his son and for a brief moment the world came to a stop. Time stood still as his son's beautiful brown eyes gazed up at him. Rico managed a half smile for an instant and then winked at his father, as he had so often seen his father do to him. The ocean breeze lightly rustled his dark brown bangs as he stared lovingly at his father.

But the moment they shared quickly came to an abrupt halt. It had been the calm before the storm, for all at once pandemonium ensued.

The boat, besieged with a barrage of massive blows—relentlessly hit time and time again—was not holding up very well. By this time, the rest of Ricardo's family, violently awakened from their slumber, was screaming hysterically. Sadly, the lone oar that Ricardo used was not enough to make any headway.

The sharks could easily claim their prize at any time, but seemed to be in no great hurry. They played with the small boat, wanting the hunt to last as long as possible. They could have harvested their bounty at any time. It was a cruel game of cat and mouse, and Ricardo recognized his beloved family was the mouse. He had no other choice, but to fight back. His family would likely perish, but he would not let them go without a fight. He began lashing out at the sharks with the oar, but it was no use; they kept coming back for more. There were just too many of them and they were too overpowering for such a small craft.

Ricardo instructed his family to stay low in the boat, but it was nearly impossible for them to hold their balance under such an attack. Without warning, the boat was struck full force, throwing them forcefully to one side. Ricardo landed on top of his wife and infant daughter. Rising at once, he sensed something was amiss.

"Rico!" Ricardo screamed, as he whipped around frantically searching for his little boy. He was no longer in the boat! Looking overboard on one side and then on the other, Ricardo cried, "Rico! No! Please, Lord, no! Ricooooo!" There was no sign of his son, only bloodstained water and the massive darkness below where the sharks had taken him.

"Rico! Rico!" Reesa screamed over and over, tightly clutching her crying daughter to her bosom. Ricardo lost any trace of reality at this point. He threw everything in the boat, including all their supplies, at the sharks. It was useless, he knew, but there was nothing else for him to do.

The boat, now rapidly filling with cold seawater, had taken all the abuse it possibly could. Ricardo and his wife huddled in the small vessel, holding their baby daughter between them. One end of the boat had sunk low into the water, sending them scrambling to the other end. A lone shark managed to work its way onto the submerged end. Ricardo faced his deadly foe, as grim black eyes bore a hole through his soul. He wildly kicked at its snout, while at the same time attempting to miss its hideous snapping jaws. More sharks fought their way into the sinking watercraft. Ricardo and Reesa stood up in what little space they had left, raising their crying baby daughter into the air above, only prolonging the inevitable. They were backed into a corner with no hope of escape.

"I love you," Ricardo bid his wife good-bye.

"I love you," she sobbed.

Ricardo lowered their dear daughter only for a moment as they both kissed her, before slowly lifting her back up to the heavens. The desperate parents courageously fought off the sharks the best they could, but it hopeless. This was the shark's domain and they possessed supremacy.

Reesa was seized by her ankle and yanked under the water so furiously that Ricardo had no time to react.

"Reesa, nooooo!" he cried, glancing down to where she had been taken below and witnessing the furious thrashing from beneath.

In an instant, Ricardo too felt something extremely powerful clamp down on his right calf. "Aaaaaggghhhhh!" he shrieked in utter terror, valiantly stretching his body upwards to buy a little more precious life for his baby girl.

An enormous pressure jerked him under into the abyss. Losing all capabilities once he entered the dismal waters, his world quickly faded to darkness. Ricardo was savagely torn apart and eaten alive by the inhabitants of the unwelcoming sea.

Donea entered the water unfamiliar with fear; she was innocent to the world, and thankfully her life was taken quickly.

A flickering silver object slowly sank through the crimson water to rest peacefully on the ocean floor. The crucifix Ricardo wore around his neck now was the symbol of freedom for this ill-fated crew.

CHAPTER THIRTY-SIX

Amanda and Kurt were ready to get down to business. Both were fully dressed in their surgical garments, preparing for the examination and dissection. The stainless-steel counters glistened with sterility, and the pale white light created a surreal atmosphere. Amanda requested a few of the naval officers to remove the shark from the freezer and place it on the table. As she went through the process of disinfecting both the shark and the table it lay on, she noticed that even though deceased, the shark still created an uneasy feeling in the pit of her stomach. She found herself instinctually shying away from its cold eyes.

Finally alone with this eighth wonder of the world, Amanda and Kurt each felt the magnitude of their find producing adrenaline flowing freely throughout their bodies.

"Well, we've waited for this moment our entire lives," Amanda proclaimed, grinning at Kurt.

"You said it," Kurt answered, grimacing as he questioned if he should have phrased his answer differently. He'd sounded like a second year university student, rather than the world-renowned scientist that he was. He shrugged, realizing she had not even noticed anyway.

Amanda and Kurt knew what they had to do and dove in headfirst. The external data was gathered first from the six foot, four inch, 360-pound male shark of unknown origin. The entire body was completely black in color, so much so, that it was tough distinguishing where the eyes were located because they seemed to nearly blend in. The skin of the shark was rougher than that of any other shark in existence. Generally, shark's skin is as rough as sandpaper, but this outdid them all. Amanda frowned as she had the thought that the skin actually appeared to consume light. She dismissed this observation, however, as an overactive imagination.

The shark was particularly adapted for high-speed swimming. It had a conical snout, seven large gill slits, aquadynamic pectoral fins, a streamlined fusiform body, a reduced second dorsal fin, a caudal peduncle that was dorsoventrally flattened forming prominent keels on both sides strengthening the tail's power, and a lunate tail with two nearly symmetric lobes. The upper lobe was slightly larger than the lower, but it was barely noticeable as with other fast-swimming sharks. The sleek body design did resemble that of other fast moving sharks, but this shark had more muscle tone and definition.

Kurt noted the dorsal fin was very distinctive. It sloped aerodynamically upward and back towards the rear of the shark to a peak, and then descended straight downward two inches before sharply zigzagging, making two deep sharp jags. The second jag was deeper than the first before reaching the midway point of the dorsal fin.

The bite radius measured approximately 1'4"x10". The moderately triangular teeth were scientifically the icing on the cake. The numerous, slate-colored deformed teeth jutted out in every direction. They outnumbered the teeth of other sharks two-fold, not even counting the replacement teeth that lined the inner jaw. The teeth themselves measured to a maximum of 1.1 inch long with razor sharp points and serrated edges that curved moderately inward at the bottom at either end of the tooth. This meant they could be used to hold a victim from escaping, very much the same way a barbed fishing hook worked.

Amanda and Kurt took notes and recorded all findings on video and audio equipment. As they finally readied themselves for dissection, Kurt was so excited he felt himself trembling. He was at odds in his feelings about this find—on the one hand, happy to be involved in such a groundbreaking landmark find, on the other hand feelings of guilt for being so joyful over something that had claimed so many lives. He kept it to himself, but pondered whether Amanda felt the same way.

Kurt would be surprised to find that she actually did share many of the same feelings he had. It was a dream come true—a life-altering event—she, however, also had feelings of tremendous guilt. How could she be so excited when others were dying because of these sharks? She looked across the table at Kurt and smiled under her surgical mask, as she asked, "Are you ready?"

"More than you'll ever know," he answered whole-heartedly, as he pushed the instrument table closer to Amanda and stood ready to assist her.

Kurt took a deep breath and handed her the scalpel. Amanda positioned the knife on the underbelly of the shark where the stomach was located. She pressed the blade against the skin, not yet penetrating the shark. She paused a moment, sweat beading on her forehead and her insides tightening up in anticipation at what she might find within.

Kurt was also nervous, apprehensive at what he was about to see. Sensing that she too felt as he did, he reached over and took Amanda's hand, holding it firmly to comfort her. Amanda squeezed his hand, and then slowly let go. Forcing herself to relax, she pressed hard, making the first incision. The foul smell grew stronger as she sliced the stomach open and the innards gushed out onto the stainless steel surgical table.

Amanda and Kurt each took a step back as the contents began to separate and the body fluids drained down the trough on either side of the table. Amanda's hands slowly sunk into the deadly aggressor, pulling bits and pieces of flesh intertwined with clothing from the lifeless killer. Nothing could be made out for sure, but they could tell there was human flesh and bone fragments.

She looked away momentarily and let out a barely audible gasp. Feeling her stomach convulse and her mouth salivate uncontrollably, her knees threatened to give way. She forced herself to focus and maintain her composure.

"Are you alright?" Kurt asked, concerned as he began to sift through the stomach contents.

"Yes, I'm fine," she answered soberly.

Kurt was a bit squeamish himself and tried comforting her. "I don't think anyone is ever prepared to see something like this."

The two of them sifted through the half-digested mess, only finding slivers and chunks of human flesh and clothing, some of which were easily identifiable as swimsuit material.

"Would you like me to do the honors?" Kurt asked. It was quite a dirty job having to pull out the remaining objects from the u-shaped stomach and stomach canal.

"Sure. Be my guest. I'll start on the head," she gladly agreed.

Kurt thrust his arm into the stomach and cringed in anticipation of what he was about to find. He felt something odd and began pulling on it, gradually drawing it out, along with fish slime, blood, and rotten flesh. He extracted what resembled clothing, and smeared away the outer covering. What he could make out was in fact a hat, probably khaki. He lifted it up and revealed it to Amanda, shaking his head in disgust. She eyed it momentarily and sighed, shaking her head in sorrow.

Taking the knife, Kurt cut away the underbelly even more to take a closer look. He stuck his hand in, sliding his arm up to his elbow inside the stomach canal. Amanda, meanwhile, prepared to make her first incision to open the head. Kurt felt something large, and a lump the size of a golf ball grew in his throat. The mass felt oddly familiar in a way. Breathing hard, he felt the chill bumps rise on his head, making every hair on the back of his neck tingle. Amanda noticed Kurt's facial expressions and briskly moved to his side of the table. A few seconds later though, she wished she had stayed put as Kurt finally managed to pull the mass free.

"Oh my God!" Kurt dropped the object and scooted away from it, hitting the instrument tray. Delicate tools rhythmically chimed as they hit the concrete floor.

"Is that what I think it is?" Amanda's eyes stared at the gruesome sight, her hand flying up to cover her mouth is dismay.

Blood and stomach acid contents had already begun to melt away the features of the half-eaten human head that lay on the table before them. It resembled a man, but no positive identification could be made just yet. To Kurt, it appeared almost unreal—a gory horror movie prop.

"This is terrible!" Kurt was sick to his stomach.

"It definitely puts more emphasis on finding out what we're dealing with here before anyone else gets killed," Amanda stated, trying not to let the sight get to her. She was a doctor after all; she had seen horrible things in her career. Obviously, this topped them all, but she was a strong person and a top professional in her field. She had to be tough and thick-skinned, even though deep down she was more than disturbed.

Amanda continued her work on the shark's head as Kurt placed the man's badly decomposed head into a glass container, filled it with formaldehyde to stop the decomposing process, and sealed it, placing it in the cooler. Everything was extensively documented and logged so as not to leave any detail out that could aid them with this discovery.

"Amanda, I think that's all from the digestive system," Kurt said, setting their minds at ease against any more grisly surprises.

"That was enough," she said sarcastically, not toward Kurt, but rather at the grave situation.

Kurt continued dissecting the creature, observing the anatomical similarities common to all species of sharks. There were also some major differences; more muscle tone, or dark muscle, which made the shark able to swim faster at a higher body temperature than the surrounding water. For its length, the shark should have been about forty pounds lighter, but the density of the muscle tissue created the extra weight. The dark muscle generated its own heat to warm the cold blood from the gills, making this shark able to swim continuously at a considerable cruising speed. It also had a highly complex digestive system, making it able to process foods at a much quicker rate than other sharks.

"This animal must stay hungry all the time," Kurt mumbled under his breath.

"Kurt? Come here and take a look at this." Amanda sounded very intrigued and the crinkled lines between her eyebrows conveyed the gravity of the matter.

Kurt swiftly made his way to the shark's head and gazed perplexed at Amanda's findings.

"Isn't it amazing?" Amanda continued. "This is going to blow the oceanographic world, or better yet the whole world, right off the map!"

"Astonishing! This can't be! I guess nothing surprises me about this creature anymore," Kurt said, shaking his head, flabbergasted at ever turn.

They were overwhelmed at the intellectual possibilities this new species of shark might possess. The brain was much larger and seemed to be more complex than that of other sharks. For that matter, a dolphin's brain, which was supposed to possess a higher capacity for intellect, paled in comparison. However, that hypothesis was just what it was—a hypothesis—until further research was performed.

"This shark could quite possibly have the power of abstract thought," Kurt said, thinking of the implications, assuming that were true. The other senses, such as the Ampullae of Lorenzini or the pores in the head that detect minute electric fields, the nostrils, and the auditory capsule were also all more highly developed when compared to other sharks.

"Just think if they possess intelligence and reasoning, far superior to that of any other life form other than humans. It could mean disaster to those inhabiting the water," Amanda hypothetically wondered out loud.

"Yes, but what makes them tick? Sharks don't just hunt and kill humans just for the sake of killing them. It's not like they are mistaking them for food, or we are invading their territory. There's got to be some explanation for all this." Kurt sounded a little distressed.

"These aren't your ordinary sharks. We don't even know where they came from. I think we need to locate their origins and study them in their own environment, if possible. I'd like to capture one alive at the very least, and I mean yesterday," Amanda stipulated adamantly.

This shark shared some of the same characteristics with other sharks, yet its unique characteristics were well advanced, distinct from that of any other shark known to man. Both Kurt and Amanda knew there would have to be more extensive research completed to place these sharks into the correct order, or to know if they would have to create a new one altogether.

Kurt opened his mouth to speak, but two naval officers abruptly entering the room cut him short. The female officer spoke to them, holding her hand over her mouth and nose so as not to breathe in the atrocious stench. "Excuse me Doctors, Admiral Wildey would like to speak with the two of you as soon as possible. The Admiral has scheduled a press conference in forty-five minutes and would very much appreciate for you to brief him on your findings before presenting them to the media."

"Ok, we'll be ready soon. Just give us a couple of minutes. There are a few things we would like for him to see," Kurt answered, gathering the data.

CHAPTER THIRTY-SEVEN

The grueling one-hour press conference seemed like five, and it left both Amanda and Kurt feeling mentally drained and empty inside. They did their best to predict the questions the press would ask, but there were always those inquiries to which both felt woefully inadequate to answer. To those questions, they did not pretend to have the answers, nor did they give any definitive responses. They simply needed more time to study this shark; of course, the media's impatience did not help matters much.

*　　*　　*

Amanda and Kurt were definitely more at ease out on the ocean than they were in front of the media. The deep emerald body and frothy white crests of the water seemed to put them both at ease, creating a single-minded purpose in the scientists' minds. They were on a mission far greater than simply scientific study. People's lives were at stake, and they both realized the importance of learning more about these creatures.

They were cruising at top speed aboard the Malangus, headed for the area where they had last seen the sharks the day before. They had finished their work on the dead shark, and Shane, along with other marine biologists, were busy performing mundane, but necessary tests and experiments back at Cathelley Naval Base.

"Kurt, are you worried we might lose power like last time?" Amanda asked, her naturally curious mind replaying their last trip out on the boat.

"The possibility is there, of course, but the way I see it, we really have no other choice, but to use the Malangus; we need its technology. Besides, the mechanics went over the entire boat from top to bottom and said there was absolutely nothing wrong it. The thing that worries me is really why we lost power in the first place. What are the chances of that happening again though?" He cracked a smile, hoping to convince Amanda that everything would be all right.

Amanda watched the evening sky advance, remembering when she was a child how she waited to hear the sizzle of the hot sun as it touched the cool water just as it dipped below the horizon, thus signaling the world it was about to leave them to the darkness. She shivered and shook off a chill; she did not like the thought of being out here with the sharks. There was no reason to worry though, she told herself. The Navy and Coast Guard were monitoring their every move and they were in constant radio contact. But a small part of her could not shake the foreboding feeling that things could easily change in the matter of an instant.

Amanda stood shoulder to shoulder with Kurt as the Malangus pressed forward into the twilight. She could feel the tight muscles flex beneath Kurt's skin as he balanced himself against the choppy ocean. In her peripheral vision, she could see Kurt's chiseled face as he gazed forward, guiding the craft into the unknown, finding herself longing to know everything about him—his childhood, past loves, favorite foods. No detail about his life seemed insignificant at that moment. She wondered if there would ever be a time for them, but knew for certain that right now was definitely not it.

CHAPTER THIRTY-EIGHT

Meanwhile, in the area known as the Bermuda Triangle the sharks could sense there was more activity than usual. They could feel the vibrations of larger ships and knew they could not prevail against this opponent. Somehow, they recognized that now, if only momentarily, they had become the hunted. The beasts felt no fear, but were smart enough to realize they would suffer substantial losses if they engaged their prey now. There was a time and a place for everything, and at this time, instinct dictated a tactical retreat.

To the sharks, it was not a question of whether or not they would win the survival game, but at what point in time their victory would take place.

CHAPTER THIRTY-NINE

"Officer Melvan spotted an unidentified object in the waters some two hundred yards portside," announced the officer to Captain Sader, who had just taken the first bite of an open-faced roast beef sandwich from the ship's mess hall.

The captain dropped his fork, rolling his eyes. "It never fails," he said to no one in particular, looking forlornly at his dinner. "All men to their positions. Sound the alarm!" Captain Sader commanded in his no nonsense manner as he pushed back from the table. The slow whine of the alarm sounded and the ship came to life in a moment's notice.

Captain Sader rushed to the deck and was met by Officer Melvan. "Captain Sader, sir, one hundred yards portside, possibly the hull of a small vessel, sir." He handed the night vision binoculars to the captain and stood ready for his orders. Captain Sader peaked through the eyelets and surveyed the area, honing in on what appeared to be the hull of a small boat. He turned the rotating knob at the top to focus the binoculars for a better view.

"I think you're right Melvan. Good spot," the Captain praised the eager young crewmember. Not looking away from the binoculars, Captain Sader sternly ordered Officer Melvan, "Announce that we are now on yellow alert."

"Aye aye Captain!" Melvan saluted and darted off to carry out his orders.

After the announcement of the alert, the officers of the U.S.C.G. Ashley prepared for their mission. They each had a specific duty to perform and they waited diligently to do so. It would be a well-practiced routine for these sailors. The giant spotlights were turned on and beamed in the direction of the object ominously bobbing up and down with the motion of the waves. The Ashley was within close range, and the sailors on deck could see that, in fact, it was a capsized boat of some kind. The highly concentrated light beams from the spotlight lit up the surface of the water, exposing an algae-riddled blue hull, which looked to be from an older, small-sized fishing boat.

"All off!" Captain Sader bellowed the command. "I want quiet on my ship—do you hear me? QUIET!" Within sixty seconds, the normally bustling vessel became as silent as a ghost ship. The engines stopped their incessant roar. No one moved. The Charleston drifted quietly in the direction of the capsized boat. Captain Sader tilted his head in an awkward manner as if to tune his hearing to any sounds that may be coming from the vessel. The only sound that could be heard, though, was the creaking of the small craft straining against the sea. The Captain waited a few moments more, but heard nothing out of the ordinary.

"All up!" Captain Sader shouted with authority. The ship came back to life in an instant, as if he had simply pressed pause on the ship's remote control, and then just as effortlessly, had released the button.

"You know the drill," the Captain barked.

Four men suddenly appeared on deck of the Ashley dressed in scuba gear, awaiting instructions. "You know what we have to do!

Let's get it done!" The divers were reluctant to go out, but they had their orders. Besides, what were the chances of those same sharks still being around?

Captain Sader examined the look of the desolate boat as the divers readied themselves to enter the water below.

There's no way sharks could have done that damage. It just isn't possible—or was it? As the captain of this ship, he was responsible for every last soul on board. Suddenly, he was reluctant to send his men into the water, but he had no other alternative. It was their duty to protect the waters off the coast. They radioed their coordinates and another Coast Guard vessel was on its way to assist.

The Captain watched as one by one his men entered the dangerous water and disappeared into the abyss to investigate the overturned boat. The entire crew kept their eyes glued on the waters surrounding the boat, waiting for their comrades to break the water's surface and give them some news.

"Shark! Shark!" came a scream from the stern. Everyone turned toward the officer, who pointed downward on the starboard side while spotlights were aimed in the vicinity. The Captain and his officers ran to the other side to see the oncoming danger. There was a lone shadow, dark and menacing, of a seven-foot shark, quickly approaching the U.S.C.G. Ashley.

"Open fire!" the Captain ordered. Several of the men fired, but missed as the shark slyly disappeared under their ship. The officer manning the spotlight that lit the wreck had already flashed the lights as a warning signal of an emergency to the divers. They were to resurface as soon as possible. The crew ran to the other side of the deck and waited for the shark to come into view, but it did not appear. Without delay, spotlights circled the entire ship desperately searching for the unseen killer of the deep. They waited, and still nothing.

"Men, keep a sharp lookout, but take care not to shoot your comrades if you see anything!" Captain Sader ordered before his men frantically grabbed their rifles and took their positions about the ship.

"Where is this devil fish hiding?" the Captain howled after several minutes ticked slowly by. As if the shark had been waiting for just such a question, a lone diver frantically rose from the depths, a shadowy stalker on his trail. He had barely broken the surface, only to scream as he was seized and quickly yanked into the darkness of the sea below; nothing could be seen, but the bubbles of air expelled from his oxygen tank. The crew stood paralyzed, not able to move or say anything.

"Hold your fire?" The words left the Captain's lips, but he instantly second-guessed his own decision, wondering if it had been wise. "You might hit one of our men," he continued, his voice uncharacteristically trailing off in indecision.

The utter stillness gave way momentarily as the lifeless wrecked boat began to shake sporadically; something was not right. There was chaotic activity within the interior of the small boat as massive amounts of air bubbles were released from its underside. The hull slowly disappeared from sight. The boat went down and there was nothing the crew on board could do but watch helplessly.

The Captain and his men could only barely make out the multitude of dark shadows zigzagging below in the murky cloud of blood. The sharks fearlessly swarmed the waters below in search of more prey. These cold-blooded murderers had effortlessly taken the lives of the Captain's own men right from under his very nose. He had been outsmarted and was now seething in rage. All he could do was unload his rifle on them, and so he did. His men joined in the brigade, muzzle flashes from the rifles and pistols lighting up the entire area surrounding the Ashley. The sulfurous smell of newly fired gunpowder permeated the air and stung the nasal passages of the crew. There was no hope of killing the slippery predators for they had already disappeared out of sight to the depths far below.

Captain Sader yelled to one of his men, "Follow them—now!" He reached the control room, short-winded, and immediately viewed the sonar. "Turn her to starboard! The sharks are getting away!"

CHAPTER FORTY

Amanda and Kurt had been monitoring the radio intently and knew of the unfortunate events that had taken place. They headed in that direction, hoping to be of help, but still had a ways to go. The Malangus was a fast ship, but at that moment it felt painfully slow to Amanda and Kurt.

"They lost them," Kurt said angrily. "Isn't that just our luck? Can anything else possibly go wrong?"

"Nothing ceases to amaze me anymore," added Amanda. "Those sharks are cunning creatures. Their intelligence level far surpasses my original assessment."

Glancing down at the compass, she exclaimed, "Oh no! Kurt, take a look at this!"

Kurt stared at the compass, head slightly cocked to one side, as it spun out of control. "Not again!" he cried, throwing his hands into the air in frustration.

Without delay, Kurt picked up the mike and radioed to anyone who happened to be listening. "Mayday, mayday. Come in Navy or Coast Guard—ANYONE! This is Dr. Wyatt of the Malangus."

There was a brief pause, but only static could be heard with the faintest crackle of a solitary voice fading in and out. Kurt tried again, "This is Dr. Kurt Wyatt of the Malangus. Can anyone hear me?" He waited impatiently for a few moments, but the constant static remained unbroken.

"It's happening again," Amanda said apprehensively, looking to Kurt for assurance. "The power will be going next," she said nervously, "and we'll be stuck here for who knows how long."

Kurt was alarmed too, but he knew he had to think rationally and keep his composure. "No, it can't be the same thing. It can't be happening again."

The lights flickered as the engine began to sputter, sounding as if it were running out of fuel. Kurt angrily hit the controls with his balled up fist, as if that would make a difference. The engine finally died, leaving them to the darkness and the harsh reality of helplessness. The ship's momentum carried the Malangus forward a bit before slowly lulling to an aimless rest. Kurt stared blankly into the nothingness surrounding him and his lovely companion.

What are we supposed to do now?

*   *   *

An hour passed while Amanda and Kurt did nothing, but wait helplessly as the Malangus slowly rocked in the gentle waves. They found some candles to chase the impenetrable darkness away and laid out a blanket on the deck to sit on while they waited either for someone to find them or for the power to return. Kurt decided against dropping the anchor for the hope of drifting to safety or, at the very least, out of the Triangle's borders.

With his back leaning against the ship's interior wall, Kurt sat on the deck, happily listening to Amanda's soft-spoken voice as she kept up a running dialogue, trying to keep their minds off the bad situation in which they were trapped. He knew she was nervous. Even he was nervous; the situation demanded as much. However, he also recognized her courage as she kept her fear from becoming overwhelming.

"…so my dad nursed the poor broken starfish back to health. I think that's where my love of the sea comes from, all the time I spent at the ocean with him, joining in on his quests, as he called them."

As she told him tales of her past, Kurt watched Amanda closely, putting to memory every facial expression, every detail of her mannerisms as the candlelight danced along her high cheekbones and played in her hair. She was stunning, the kind of stunning that won beauty contests, but Kurt knew the way a woman looked on the outside was not really what made her beautiful, at least not to him. It was her heart, her soul, her mind, and all the little idiosyncrasies that made her unique that had drawn Kurt's heart to Amanda. Her looks were only icing on the cake.

He toyed with the idea of making a declaration of his feelings for her, but the dangerous situation they were in kept him silent. It was not the right time; it was never the right time it seemed. He vowed to himself that if they made it off this boat alive, he would tell her how he felt about her the second their feet hit the dock.

Amanda's auburn hair was pulled into a loose French braid down the back of her head, small strands of her hair mischievously escaping to brush against her brow. This obviously annoyed her and, without thinking, she smoothed them back into place repeatedly, reminding Kurt of his beloved wife as she had done the same. He smiled broadly in the dark as memories of Miranda crashed into his conscious thought; she had been another beautiful woman on the inside, as well as on the outside.

While most of his friends seemed to be on a marriage merry-go-round, marrying and divorcing like it was an annual event, such as the Thanksgiving Day Parade, Kurt and Miranda's love had been something special right from the beginning. Even when times were rough, they were on solid ground, happily making the sacrifices and putting in the daily work of keeping their relationship in harmony.

As Kurt delved deeper into his memories, he realized that some of the days he and Miranda thought were the worst had actually become fond memories over the years, such as the Christmas he had set the kitchen on fire trying to help Miranda make dinner for her parents. They had thought it was the worst disaster they'd ever had; the entire kitchen had to be gutted. But in retrospect, they had never liked the kitchen anyway and they had great fun together redesigning it to fit their needs.

Yes, the good days had far outweighed the bad days—there just had not been enough of them. When his wife died, Kurt would have given up every single thing to have only one more minute with her.

So why was he wasting precious minutes now, waiting for the perfect time to tell Amanda how he felt? Time, he understood far too well, was a commodity that once gone was irretrievable forever.

Kurt realized Amanda had gone quiet, and he looked up from his introspection, only to find the spot where she had been lounging was now empty. How long had he been lost in thought? Alarmed, he came quickly to his feet.

"Amanda?" he breathed as his eyes darted, looking from one shadow to the next in the darkness. His mind immediately going to the worst possible scenario in panic, he whispered, "The water…" Leaning as far over the railing as he dared, he searched the pitch-black water below to no avail. He could see nothing. He listened carefully, but the sea sounded calm. His mind, though, was terror-stricken by what he'd seen in the stomach of that shark earlier.

Where else could she be? There was only one way he could be sure she had not gone overboard unnoticed.

He pulled himself up, precariously perching on the side of the boat. *If only there was some moonlight tonight…* Squinting into the darkness, he prepared to jump.

"Kurt Wyatt, what do you think you're doing?"

He turned and saw Amanda at the edge of the flickering candlelight, holding a steaming mug in each hand. She held one out toward him, "I managed to make some tea. Thank goodness, the burners run on propane. Whatever are you doing, anyway?"

Relief rushed through Kurt's body at the sight of her, safe and sound. He jumped down and grabbed her, hugging her tightly, spilling tea all over the deck in the process.

"Don't ever scare me like that again," he scolded, fear evident in his tone. "What would I have done if I'd lost you when I've just found you? I've been so stupid for keeping my feelings to myself. I was so scared. I love you and never want to… "

"You—you love me?"

He tightened his hold on her, wishing he could hold her like this for the rest of his life. "I do."

Amanda's heart soared. She wanted to wrap her arms around him and let him know she felt the same, but continued to hold the mugs out to the side, not having any other recourse. Instead, she simply laid her head against his chest, grinning at the sound of his racing heart.

"I do too."

CHAPTER FORTY-ONE

Suddenly a jarring crash came from the bow of the Malangus.

"What now?" Kurt muttered as he violently jolted awake. He tensed momentarily, not immediately recognizing his surroundings. Looking down, he smiled at Amanda, remembering only hours before as he had made an impulsive declaration of love to her. His arms had been wrapped around her as she slept against his chest, but now she sat up, rubbing the sleep from her eyes and trying to focus in the still darkness around them. The candles had all burnt out, leaving the pair squinting against the dark night.

"What was that?" Amanda asked sleepily, slowly stretching her arms over her head and watching Kurt get to his feet.

"I don't know," Kurt answered, "I'm going to have to go inside to grab the high intensity flashlight. Hopefully, it still has some charge to it. You stay put; don't move a muscle."

Kurt came back several minutes later, a sharp, but flickering beam of light preceding him. He leaned over the side of the boat slightly and moved the light in a sweeping fashion, quickly finding the problem. Another boat, now nestled against the Malangus, had also lost power, and possibly its crew, as well.

"Hello!" Kurt shouted. "Is anyone aboard?" He was somehow not surprised when nothing was heard, but the lapping of the sea and the creaking of the other ship. He felt Amanda brush up against him. Startled, he turned, smiling as she wrapped her arms around him from the back.

"What is it?" she asked.

"We've collided with a fishing boat. Thank God, we were both adrift or who knows what might have happened," Kurt pointed out as he pointed at the boat by shining the flashlight at it. "The boat seems to be in the same predicament we are—no power. Oddly, it doesn't seem anyone is aboard, but I probably should make sure. Someone could be hurt."

"Is there anything you need me to do?"

"Try to find more candles, or something to make a torch with. There should be some oily rags and gas in the engine compartment. I have the lighter," Kurt dug in his pocket "Here it is. I need to investigate the other boat, so I'll need to take the flashlight with me. This light is already flickering though. Who knows how long it will hold out?"

No more that a second later, the light noticeably dimmed before going out altogether. Kurt shook it, and then smacked it against his leg. "Of course, we'd have no luck at all if it wasn't for bad luck."

"I guess this discussion was well-timed, at least," Amanda chuckled, before setting out for the engine compartment to gather the materials. On the way down, she grabbed a small mop and broom. Upon arriving in the engine compartment, she unscrewed the heads of both, leaving only the handles. As Kurt had indicated, she swiftly located a couple of oily rags and doused them with gasoline. She then tightly wrapped the rags around the end of each handle, and then raced back to Kurt.

During her absence, Kurt rustled up some rope and grabbed the Ruger P-95 handgun he kept in a lock-box in a storage compartment on deck. The gun was always fully loaded just for this kind of emergency. He met Amanda at the top of the stairs and she handed him the two torches.

"Here you go," Amanda said. "Now what?"

"That was quick. Resourceful, aren't you?" Kurt grinned, taking each handle and, using his knee as leverage, snapped them both in two, making the torches shorter and easier to maneuver. He struck his lighter and held it to the cloth, which immediately burst into a small flame. "You keep the other with you. Do you know how to use one of these?" Kurt asked, handing her the Ruger.

"I sure do," she teased, as she confidently cocked and checked the safety. "But do you really think I'll need it?" She looked at him, concerned.

"There's no telling what will happen. We could be getting hijacked, for all I know. So, just to be on the safe side, keep it. I have a derringer tucked under my belt," Kurt cautioned her.

At the bow of the Malangus, they observed the other boat had drifted a little. Kurt tied one end of a thick, waterproof nylon rope to the Malangus. He then reared back, heaving the rest of the rope toward the shrimp boat, grunting as it left his hand and landed squarely on the other boat's deck.

He turned to Amanda and hesitated before placing his arm around her waist and pulling her to him. He gently pressed his lips against hers, reassuring her that he would be back as soon as he could.

"Be careful," Amanda said, concern making her voice sound tight.

"Wish me luck," Kurt said, trying to calm any fears with his smile. He climbed onto the railing, and Amanda watched him leap almost four feet across the water, just barely making it to the other boat. He tucked and rolled, hitting something on the deck and howling in pain as he came to an abrupt stop against some netting.

He quickly surveyed the darkness as he tried to focus on his surroundings. The light from the small torch danced ominously about him, creating shadows that gave Kurt the spooks. He winced as he desperately rubbed the pain in his back. He had landed on a pole or pipe, deeply bruising his back. He held his torch outward as he searched for his rope. He finally spotted it. Sticking the handle end of the torch in the nearby netting, he pulled up the slack between the two boats before tying the rope firmly to the stern.

"Kurt! Are you alright?" Amanda yelled.

"Yes, I'm tying her up now," Kurt shouted back to the silhouette of Amanda on the Malangus. He was concerned for her safety, and wanted to get to the bottom of this and get back to her as soon as possible.

Lumbering across the deck to retrieve his torch, he noticed that everything on the vessel was in total disarray. There were dead shrimp and other sea creatures, still entangled in the nets, and the pole used to haul in the nets had been broken off and was nowhere to be seen. It appeared as though whoever had been on board was in the middle of fishing when something went drastically wrong.

Holding the torch tightly before him to light the way downstairs, he noticed nothing out of the ordinary. He pulled out his derringer and cocked it, holding it close to his side. It was only good for two shots at close range, but it would do some damage, and it was all he had. He cautiously descended down each step. His outreached hand fumbled the small torch, not exactly helping in his exploration. He could only see a few feet and then there was darkness.

As he slowly went down the stairs and gasped, jumping back up one step as his foot splashed into something cold and wet. The ship was taking in water!

Carefully stepping back into the frigid water, he grit his teeth as he made his way to the bottom of the steps. The water level crested just above his knees, as he waded through the old boat, surveying the one room cabin. There were two cots completely submerged underwater, and other furniture and belongings floated about the cabin. Slowly wading through the water, letting each foot cautiously explore its surroundings, he was careful not to injure himself. He stopped, slightly turning his head to one side—he heard something; he was sure of it! He listened intently, shaking his head as he heard no sound, so he continued around the room looking for some type of evidence or answers to the owner's whereabouts.

He studied the decor as best he could in the flickering light, noticing that the ship was pretty old, but still in good shape for its age. He continued on, abruptly stopping to listen. He heard the same faint, rustling sound. He was sure of it this time. Turning in the direction of the noise, he followed it. Holding the derringer in his sweaty grip, he edged toward the closet door, following the sound.

Kurt prepared himself for battle. His heart pumped enough blood for five men, and he had to steady himself against the dizziness. He cautiously grabbed the handle and turned it, pulling open the door a few inches. Unable to stand the anticipation any longer, he violently whipped the door open all the way, nearly tearing the hinges off in the process. He thrust the torch into the closet, all the while holding the derringer in front of him for protection. A high-pitched scream came from inside the closet and Kurt nearly let a shot go before catching himself. There on a shelf, just above the water, huddled a little girl. Her hands covered her eyes from fear, as well as the glare of the torch flame.

"Are you alright?" Kurt asked surprised but relieved, but she didn't answer. "It's ok. I'm going to help you."

Kurt tried reaching out for her, but she pulled away from him. "Sweetie, we need to get out of here. The ship is sinking and we've got to go!" Despite Kurt's reassuring tone, she would neither budge nor look in his direction. He knew from the way she trembled that the girl was in shock. Something horrible happened here, he thought, but his first priority was to get the both of them off this vessel to safety. He tucked the gun under his belt on his backside and hesitantly reached for the girl with one hand.

"Now honey, we need to get out of here," his voice became slightly firmer as the urgency increased. "I'm your friend and I want to help you."

The water was still rising higher, so he grabbed the back of her bibbed overalls, and she surprisingly jumped to his chest and held him in a frightened bear hug. A warm feeling flooded over him as he trudged for the stairs holding onto the frightened child. He reached the deck and tried setting the girl down, but had no luck. She was too scared and did not want to be left alone. Her legs and arms were wrapped around him, holding on for dear life, and at times Kurt found it difficult to breath.

"Is there anyone else aboard?" Kurt asked softly, realizing the little girl must have gone through something traumatic. She still would not answer. Kurt pried her head from his chest and looked into her eyes intently.

"Listen, I need to know. It's important you tell me." She looked down shyly, but Kurt gently pulled her face back up to meet his sincere, but somber eyes. She paused for a moment before slowly shaking her head no.

"Ok honey, I'm going to take you to my boat and we're going to get you home." He smiled at her, but her face was blank, void of any emotion. "By the way, my name is Kurt. What is yours?"

"Lisha," she mumbled against his shoulder.

"What was that? I couldn't hear you?" Kurt asked again.

She lifted her head from his shoulder and whispered, "Alisha."

"That's a very pretty name," Kurt said, trying to gain her trust. "I'm going to take you to my boat where you'll be safe. I have a friend there, and I know she'll be very happy to see you."

Kurt carried Alisha to where the two boats met and stuck the torch back into a ball of netting.

"Amanda!" Kurt shouted.

"Kurt?" she answered, puzzled at his distorted image. "Did you find anything? What are you holding?"

"You're not going to believe this. I found a little girl," he pulled the rope's slack, bringing the boats together. He had no worries about dropping the girl. She held on so tightly, she was not going anywhere.

"You what?" she said knowing that she heard him correctly the first time. "Is she alright?"

"As far as I can tell she'll be fine, but I think she's in shock though. I'm not sure what happened here, but there is no one else aboard and the boat is taking in water." Kurt was now close enough to see Amanda clearly.

"Alisha, this is my friend Amanda. She is going to take you now, so you have to let go, honey. I'm going to hand you to her. Are you ready?" Kurt asked calmly.

"Yes," she whispered, her barely audible voice making Kurt's heart drop.

Amanda stretched over the side of the Malangus as Kurt hoisted Alisha up and over to her waiting arms. They disappeared from Kurt's sight as Amanda sat the little girl on the deck. He could faintly hear Amanda's soothing tones as she mothered the frightened child.

Without warning, blows rocked the broken vessel and sent Kurt hurtling towards the water. He desperately reached out for anything within reach and, luckily, grabbed hold of the rope that tied the two vessels together. He was still precariously submerged up to his chest in the sea though, and something deep within the recesses of his mind told him to get out of the water as quickly as he could. It had to be those sharks and he was not about to be next on their menu. Racing to pull himself out of the water, he held on to the slippery rope for dear life as he pulled himself hand over hand up the rope. He scrutinized the dark waters below, half expecting to see his death quickly coming for him. He knew in his gut something was down there.

The waters below began to splurge with life. The shadows told him his instincts had, indeed, been correct. They were down there and they wanted blood—his blood. He heard Amanda screaming over all of the confusion and it motivated to pull himself the rest of the way onto the Malangus.

Kurt lay on the deck, soaking wet and gasping huge gulps of air in complete exhaustion. He could not get enough oxygen to fill his lungs. His head rested on Amanda's lap and she comforted him soothingly.

The bombardment once aimed at the shrimp boat, now turned dreadfully to the Malangus. Kurt regained his energy the best he could and pried himself from the comfort of Amanda's lap. All at once the Malangus pulled to one side, sending them rolling, end over end, to the other side of the deck. Amanda managed to get up first and stared out into the night.

"Kurt, the other boat is sinking and …" Amanda started to speak.

"It's pulling us under with it!" Kurt yelled, finishing her sentence.

"I'll be right back. Hang on!" Kurt disappeared momentarily, but returned quickly brandishing an axe. "Stand clear!"

He balanced himself, drawing back the axe and swinging it, cutting the rope halfway.

"Come on!" he roared, swinging again, this time making contact through the rope and hitting the metal pole where it was tied. Sparks flew in the darkness. The Malangus bobbed to and fro until it balanced itself into normal buoyancy. Kurt looked out over the water, but the shrimp boat was now history—nowhere to be found. The Malangus was not in the clear yet though, as the sharks still besieged them.

"Are you and Alisha ok?" Kurt asked, checking on them through the shadowy gray tones of the diminishing night.

"Yes, I guess we're as well as can be expected, given the circumstances," Amanda answered, while hastily fitting a lifejacket onto Alisha. The blows by their tormentors slowed and, surprisingly, eventually stopped. Only silence and the movements of the water could be heard.

Kurt joined Amanda as they dejectedly watched the ominous shark fins encircling the Malangus.

"You know they're just taunting us, don't you?" Amanda murmured, to which Kurt nodded in agreement. "Like a cat plays with a mouse before... killing it." Amanda's voice slowly trailed off into silence. They turned to see Alisha blankly staring at them.

"They won't go away," Alisha said, matter-of-factly, her eyes staring right through Kurt and Amanda.

"They'll never go away."

CHAPTER FORTY-TWO

"I have orders from the President, sir," Admiral Wildey's voice crackled over the radio. "We're to employ ATW missiles on those monsters. We'll all be eating sushi for dinner for the next two weeks."

"Wildey, do you know what will happen to the sea life and the ecology if we use that powerful of explosives?" the Admiral said, gritting his teeth to hold back his anger. Admiral Norge was a prudent, caring man, but the Navy was testing his patience. After all, the Coast Guard had never gotten the respect it deserved—especially from Navy personnel.

"Sir, I can assure you we have taken everything into consideration," the Navy Admiral continued, boastfully. "We will take all the necessary precautions to minimize the impact to the surrounding area." He paused. "I think you will agree these sharks are likely to inflict far more devastation on the underwater world, and on mankind for that matter, than this one-time blow of an explosive charge. We have no other alternative. We've exhausted all other avenues in dealing with these creatures. You know what we're up against here, sir. If killing those things out there means we have to waste a few leatherback turtles in the process, then I say the turtles lose... so be it! It's a matter of survival, sir."

"I suppose you're right," Norge reluctantly agreed. "Are precautions being taken not to detonate with other vessels in the vicinity?"

"Yes sir, our aircraft and fleet are equipped with state-of-the-art military technology. So, if the Coast Guard finds those sharks before we do—just let us know. We're as good as there!"

"Will do, Admiral; you have our complete cooperation," Norge said, doubtfully. He wrestled with the thought of the massive destructive power from explosives of that magnitude, but they had not found another option that worked.

Is there any other way? He rethought the options, but in the end he had to agree with the Navy Admiral. These sharks, or whatever they were, had to be stopped, no matter the cost. None could survive—not a single one of them. All ideas had already been thrown on the table only to be shot down after further review from the powers that be.

"By the way Admiral, has there been any word on the Malangus?" Admiral Norge asked intently.

"No, I'm afraid not. I know just about as much as you do. We've been searching with all means possible, but even our aircraft have yet to turn up anything. Don't worry, if there out there, we'll find them."

"It's like they vanished into thin air," Norge concluded. "By the way, do Dr. Paige and Dr. Wyatt know of your plans to use those missiles?"

"No sir, they don't. This is classified military information and you understand, my orders come from the top. If and when I am instructed to release that information, I will," Wildey rebutted.

There was momentary silence on the line.

"Well, I guess that's all for now, Admiral. Again, thanks and I'll keep you abreast of the situation."

"Yes sir, same here," Commandant Norge replied, then placed the phone back into the cradle.

He slowly eased himself back into his leather chair, which crinkled with each movement of his body. He gazed at the miniature model Coast Guard ship in the bottle he had made many years ago, and finished off the rest of his hot chocolate, which had turned cold and was so sweet he cringed as it met his taste buds.

He searched his past until his mind rested quietly on the memory of his first day as a Coast Guard officer; he'd had dreams of making a difference in the world, in the sea, and the lives he would touch in his endeavors. It was hard for him to admit that taking out the sharks in that way was the best way, and he was uneasy about the decision that would wipe out life as he knew it in the sea, but he also recognized it had to be done. There was no alternative. Those killers of the deep had to be stopped, even if it meant the sacrificing thousands of sea creatures.

He was just troubled over the extent of the death and destruction, which the explosives might cause. The military already had a reputation for overkill when it came to using its weaponry and this gave him even more reason to worry. He quickly forced himself back from his daydreams and into the horrible nightmare of his reality. He had to notify his men of the plans and he could waste no time in doing so.

CHAPTER FORTY-THREE

Amanda could see the distressed look that plagued Kurt's face as he reached the deck. His white tee shirt was stained with grease and sludge from working on the engine below.

"No luck," Kurt tried to smile, managing only a weak attempt. "I'm not a mechanic, but I tried everything I know. It's dead." He motioned for Amanda to come over to him so he could speak to her in private.

She started to get up, but Alisha held on to her with a vice-like grip, refusing to let go. "It's alright, honey. I just need to talk to Kurt for a minute. I'll be right back. I promise." The child reluctantly released her hold on Amanda, and the look of complete innocence and longing on the girl's face broke Amanda's heart as she walked away.

She anticipated the bad news that was about to come from Kurt's sun-parched lips. "Well, what is it?" she gloomily asked.

"You're not going to believe this, but…" Kurt stopped in mid-sentence, unable to place his thoughts into the right words.

"Go on," she said almost sharply, wishing Kurt would just get straight to the point. "It can't get any worse, so just say it."

Kurt understood her impatience and came right out with it. "We're taking in water."

"What? You've got to be kidding me!" She almost laughed out loud at their unbelievably bad luck.

"The powerful force these sharks are capable of is unimaginable, but it's true."

"How fast is it coming in? How much time do we have before we become the soup of the day for those things," she said, interrupting him.

"Well, it's hard to really say, but the floor below has about two feet of water. As the Malangus continues to fill, the pressure will continue to increase, causing the break to grow until it eventually becomes a hole big enough to capsize us. Not to mention, there will be new damage done should those sharks begin their barrage again."

"Isn't there anything we can do to stop the leak, or at least slow it down?" Amanda's mind wrestled with every possibility.

Kurt took a deep breath and expelled the air heavily. "I don't think so," he replied.

"You know what I think? I think they're out there—waiting. They're calculating their next move. They know exactly what they're doing. Smarter than I ever imagined," Amanda ranted, somewhat hysterical and perhaps a little louder. Remembering their company, she quickly looked over her shoulder to Alisha, sighing in relief that she had not heard her.

"What I *would* like to know is, where is the Navy, the Coast Guard, or anyone else, for that matter?" Amanda asked, her fear making her angry.

"I don't know, but I hope they show up before those sharks decide it dinnertime," Kurt said, surveying the area, but finding nothing through the obscurity of night.

As if on cue, the ship began to rock and jerk, once more under attack by the vile sharks. A high-pitched scream escaped the small child's mouth, permeating the darkness as they both rushed over to her. Amanda held her tightly, rocking back and forth and softly cooing words of reassurance to her.

Kurt quickly headed below with a lit candle in hand.

"It will be alright, little one," Amanda cooed, trying to calm the little girl, even though she too was scared. She squeezed Alisha a little tighter in a feeble attempt to stop her trembling.

Kurt sprang to the deck from below with a couple of flare gun cartridges in hand. "I found a couple more flares. The last five didn't help, but hopefully these will." Kurt was very angry at his helpless situation, but he was going to do his best with what he had to work with.

Kurt methodically placed the flare cartridge in the gun, struggling to keep his balance. The sharks seemed to be attacking the Malangus with an even greater force than before.

Were they tired of the waiting game?

Did they just want to get their kill and move on?

Kurt lost his balance, falling to one knee. Crab-walking over to the side of the boat, he rested his back against it for stability. Taking a huge gulp of air, he lifted the gun, extending his arm overhead and firing the flare upward into the darkened sky above.

The flare made a hissing sound as it left the gun and continued on until it was too far away to hear anymore. The flare suddenly exploded in the night sky and the darkness was pushed back and held momentarily at bay. Using the light, Kurt searched for nearby ships or aircraft, disappointed when he found none. Looking down, he quickly surveyed the surrounding water below, falling back as the scene stunned him.

Amanda hunched down in an almost fetal position, holding Alisha, as Kurt's body language caught her attention. It was enough to leave her no illusions as to the fate of their ill-timed love story.

Amanda sprang up to glance over the railing as the light slowly faded. She could see the sight that had paralyzed Kurt. As far as she could see, the waters were infested with hundreds, possibly thousands, of the terrible black jagged fins. There were so many, thickly surrounding the boat, that some were actually out of the water writhing on the backs of the others. Their penetrating eyes made Amanda's blood run cold. They almost looked to be in competition with one another to see which could get the first taste of flesh. The light slowly flickered away, leaving Kurt and Amanda with the cold reality of hopelessness. They saw what they were up against and it made their skin crawl with fear.

Kurt knew he had to think of something fast. The Malangus was starting to sink at a much faster rate than what he had anticipated.

"Do you think if we fired a flare into the water it would scare them off?"

Amanda asked, startling Kurt. He turned to see that both girls had eased over to be closer to him. He crouched down level with them while trying to hold his balance.

"That's a thought, but it probably wouldn't work. And even if it did, it would only be a temporary fix," Kurt replied, distracted as he looked around the boat for something, anything that could save them. Unfortunately, nothing new presented itself.

"You're right, of course. If we use the flare and it doesn't work, then we have no way to signal for help." Amanda conceded, nodding her head.

Amanda was holding up pretty well, Kurt thought. Most others, whether man or woman, would have broken down and given up all hope by now. She was a strong person and Kurt admired her for that.

"Are we going to die?" Alisha quietly asked, her tear filled eyes burning a hole in Kurt's heart.

"No honey, we're going to be rescued. It's only a matter of time," Amanda promised, her voice hesitant but strong. She knew, deep down, it was going to take a miracle for them to make it out alive, but if a miracle was what they needed, then for Alisha's sake she would pray for one. After all, she had always believed in miracles. She knew better than to ever give up, even when it seemed all hope was lost.

And right then, it did, indeed, seem that all hope was lost, for the Malangus could not hold up much longer.

CHAPTER FORTY-FOUR

The minutes passed too quickly as time ran out for the little crew of the Malangus. Kurt searched the entire ship for anything and everything that would possibly help them defend themselves against their assailants. The radio was useless, and of course, the boat would never have any power again now that the engine was literally below sea level. He finally found some shells for the shotgun and he loaded it hastily. Amanda still possessed the Ruger, which unfortunately held only seven rounds. With what meager defense fortification they had, they were ready to make a stand, determined to fight to the death, if necessary.

"I know this is practically useless, but it's all we've got; besides the Ruger you have and the derringer that…" he stopped abruptly, frantically patting the back of his pants. "Does nothing ever go our way?" he hissed through clenched teeth.

"What's wrong?" Amanda asked, watching as Kurt turned every one of his pockets inside out.

"It's the derringer. Just my luck! I must have lost it when I fell in the water trying to board the Malangus from Alisha's boat."

All Amanda could do was shake her head in disbelief at their run of bad luck.

The shotgun was not likely to scare away these sharks, but Kurt knew they had no other course of action, besides just laying down and giving up. *Not on my watch*, he thought vehemently.

There were eleven shells in his pocket, as well as those already loaded into the gun, before Kurt aimed and fired blindly into the dark depths. One after another, shots rang out into the air. *Boom! Boom! Boom!* Amanda and Alisha nearly jumped out of their skins at each shot, yet they held close to one another, fearing the end was near. Amanda sheltered Alisha's ears the best she could from the noise of the gunshots, at the expense of her own hearing.

Kurt was right; it *was* useless. The shots he fired made no impact on the situation they were in. He might as well have been just tossing the shotgun shells into the water for all the good it did. He was convinced he had not killed a single shark. If anything, the shots had actually increased the beasts' commitment to destroy them.

Loading the remaining two shells into the shotgun, he leaned it against the wall and, awkwardly, made his way to the stern. The boat was listing severely down now toward the back, making movement difficult. Kurt's heart fluttered as he stepped in water, which had by now risen even with the top deck.

Disappearing just out of Amanda and Alisha's view, he quickly returned carrying a yellow box, which he laid in the middle of the deck. He had never had to use one of these before with the exception of training years ago, so he was somewhat unfamiliar with the instructions. Fumbling and pulling at the strings, he quickly jumped out of the way as an explosion startled him and the box magically transformed into a large rubberized lifeboat. One look at it, though, made it clear it was woefully inadequate for their current situation.

Amanda gave him a look that implied that he was out of his mind. "That isn't going to work. They'll bite right through that! You know they will!"

"You're probably right, but it's all we've got! Besides, it could buy us some time once the deck starts to overflow with water." He paused momentarily, not wanting to tell her how dire their situation had become, but knowing he had to. "Which it has already," he whispered, jabbing his finger in the direction of the now flooded deck.

Amanda closed her eyes, putting her head into her trembling hands and praying just under her breath for their salvation. She then took a deep breath, and calmly picked up Alisha, gently placed her in the lifeboat.

"Alisha, I'm going to help Kurt. I want you to stay here ok? I'll be right back," Amanda said reassuring her.

"No!" Alisha cried, her small hand reaching out for Amanda.

"It'll be fine sweetie. I'll be back," Amanda reassured her, not waiting for a reaction.

"How can I help?" Amanda asked.

"Grab anything you think we could use as weapons, or anything else we might need and put it in the raft. Once the Malangus goes under, whatever we have on that raft is all we'll ever have," Kurt answered grimly.

There was not much to be had from the deck, only the axe, shotgun, flare gun, the Ruger she carried tucked into her shorts, and some candles. She looked over their provisions critically. Their time on this planet was dwindling, however, they would fight for every last second of it. They were not going down easy.

The water completely blanketed the deck, and the life raft was now afloat within the confines of the boat. Kurt did not say a word, but raised his arm into the air and shot the last flare into the sky. Instantly, the world around them came alive with yellowish pale light. Unfortunately, it illuminated their sad and desperate predicament. They looked out at their situation and then slowly into one another's eyes, realizing there was no hope of survival. The dense army of sharks could easily be seen surrounding the Malangus.

"Let's just pray someone sees it," Amanda said, holding back the tears that threatened to fall.

Kurt was quiet, thinking how absurd it was that his life would end this way. He had found the woman he loved and wanted to spend the rest of his life with, and ironically, that was exactly what would happen. He would spend the rest of his life in this lifeboat with Amanda. *Well,* he decided, *if this is all the time we have together, I'm not going to waste one more minute of it.*

He looked deep into Amanda's tearful eyes, aglow with the flickering of the last industrial candle they had. If he had been able to live another fifty years, he would have never forgotten the unexpected constricting of his heart the very first time he looked into those eyes. He hugged her tightly. "I love you... so much," Kurt murmured quietly.

"I love you too," Amanda replied, and they kissed for what would be the very last time.

Breaking off the kiss abruptly, Amanda whispered, her lips still against his, "Do you hear that?"

"No, what?"

"That! Do you hear it?" She asked again, pulling away as her eyes searched the still opaque grey of night.

"I hear it!" said Alisha "What is it?"

Kurt turned to Amanda, smiling broadly. "I think it's a helicopter!"

"Will they be able to find us?" Alisha asked, hopefully.

In the distance, a low thudding sound could be heard cutting the skies above. A helicopter was scanning the waters with a high-powered searchlight on the horizon and it was heading in their direction. It was rapidly approaching, but at its current pace, Kurt doubted they would find them in time.

Thud! Something hit the Malangus' deck. It was the sound of the inevitable.

"One's onboard!" Kurt cried.

Alisha screamed in terror and buried her head into Amanda's stomach.

"Shoot him! Shoot that thing!" Amanda screamed.

Kurt readied himself for battle as he stared through the darkness for his adversary. He waited for it to make the first move, so he could blow it out of the water. Amanda held the candle out so he could see, but it was no help. Kurt heard the helicopter just overhead; nevertheless he could not take his eyes off his foe. He knew that other sharks would also make their way onto the deck and he could not afford to let that happen.

"This is the United States Coast Guard," a voice boomed over the helicopter's loudspeaker. "We are lowering our lift carrier to pull all of you aboard. Our pulley can only handle one person per trip. Buckle yourself in as fast as possible. You don't have much time."

As the light from the helicopter lit up the area, Kurt spotted the cold reflection of the shark's eyes on him. The deadly beast surged toward the raft as Kurt squeezed the trigger, ripping a hole through one side of the creature's face. It was stunned momentarily, but then it spun around in confused anger, bent on doing some damage before it died.

Kurt only had one shot left, and was not prepared for what the shark was about to do next, but Amanda was. She quickly unloaded all seven shots from the Ruger into the head of the shark, just in time. Kurt managed to fire his remaining shot, stopping the shark cold as it continued splashing toward them. It finally stopped with a heave, grazing the raft and dousing its crew. The shark floated lifelessly along side the raft.

Kurt looked to Amanda with amazed approval. "Thank goodness, you opened her up or who's telling what could have happened! I'm not going to take any chances though," Kurt said, picking up the axe and slamming it into the shark's flesh several times. If it wasn't dead before, it was now.

"Kurt, help me with the carrier!" Amanda shouted, pointing upward with urgency.

The carrier reached the raft and Kurt pulled the blood-soaked axe from the dead shark and speedily assisted Amanda and Alisha into the carrier.

"But Kurt, they said only one at a time," Amanda argued.

"We don't have time for that, besides both of you together weigh less than I do. It'll hold; trust me!" He kissed Alisha on the forehead before kissing Amanda quickly on the lips. Buckling them in tightly, he then looked upward, holding his arm up to shield his eyes from the glare. Waving his index finger in a circular motion, he signaled the crew of the helicopter it was safe to begin lifting. Amanda and Alisha swiftly flew upwards towards the safety of the Coast Guard helicopter. As the lift carried her away, Amanda turned to Kurt, wondering if she would ever see him again.

"I'm right behind you!" he optimistically called out, hoping his smile would calm Amanda's fears. The two girls stared down at him with fear as they rose higher into the night sky.

Kaapussh. Another shark splashed aboard. Kurt was well aware all he had for protection now was the axe, but he turned, ready for action, towards his aggressor and crouched down, feet wide apart to keep some stability.

More helicopters approached in the distance, but they were of no use to him now. He took his eyes from the shark for a split second, checking quickly to see that Amanda and Alisha were safely aboard. As long as they were safe, nothing else mattered.

The shark took its time circling the raft. It teased him, never getting near enough for Kurt to take a swing at it. He quickly glanced upward again and to his relief the carrier was slowly on its way back down. He only had to hold out for a few moments more. However, his relief would be short-lived, as the carrier was not moving fast enough for him to avoid a face-off with the menace that circled him.

Gracefully turning near the stern of the ship, the shark, without warning, bulleted towards Kurt. He had to make his first—and possibly last—strike count, so he reared back and waited patiently for his enemy to come into range. It was so fast Kurt nearly misjudged its speed. The shark's jaws locked onto the raft just about the same time Kurt swung the axe with all his strength, planting it squarely in the top of his opponent's head. The force of the blow sent him reeling backwards into the rising waters on the Malangus' deck. Never loosening its grip on the raft, the shark shook and thrashed about in the water violently as it died.

Unexpectedly, the Malangus dropped approximately a foot into the water; she was about to go down for the last count. The carrier hit the surface of the water almost ten yards off the mark. Other sharks succeeded getting onto the sinking boat, and Kurt would need to make his way through the shark infested water to reach the life saving basket.

He swam for his life. He was no match for these natural killing machines, and his only sanctum was to reach the carrier and hope the Coast Guard would be able to pull him up in time.

Kurt quickly looked over his shoulder one final time, only to see the jagged fins of death as they charged after him. Stroke after stroke, he feverishly pulled his body through the water until he finally reached the carrier and clumsily scrambled in, taking one last look back at his hunters as they lunged for him. He grabbed onto the cable pulling the carrier up, as he was knocked about by several of the gruesome monsters. Their heads and protruding jaws raised above the surface of the water and snapped desperately at Kurt before he swung upward into the lifesaving sky.

Kurt peered over the edge of the basket to see the multitude of sharks that swelled below. *What a phenomenon*, he thought. Even though they were ready to rip him apart, he could not help but look at them and marvel at their heightened state of development. The sharks were furious and frenzied into chaos. They appeared to literally be angry over not claiming a kill, and the more dominant of them turned against their own ranks. The scene was horrifically breathtaking.

Now that Kurt was in the air, he could see the legion of Navy choppers surrounding the perimeter. The Malangus sadly bid its fateful farewell and disappeared into the depths, once again pulling his attention below as massive air bubbles were released from below.

He quickly climbed aboard the helicopter at the top and immediately looked for the girls. He could not have anticipated a better reception.

"Kurt, thank God you're safe! We were watching the whole thing and …" Amanda cried uncontrollably, joyous tears rolling down her cheeks.

"It's ok. We're all fine now," he hugged her, and winked at Alisha, gesturing her to join them in a group hug.

"Good to have you aboard, Doctor," the Coast Guard officer that pulled him on board said, as he patted him on the shoulder. "How's life been treating you lately?" The officer asked him sarcastically, but accompanied by a smile stretching from ear to ear.

"Not too shabby," Kurt said in an equally sarcastic manner. "It's good to be aboard. I feel like just thanking you isn't enough. You saved our lives and I'm most grateful." Kurt was at a loss of what to do next, so he pulled the officer into the group hug as well.

Kurt was intrigued by the high speed at which the Coast Guard's helicopter was traveling, along with the tactical air maneuvers from the Navy choppers that he viewed from his window as he buckled himself into his seat. "Why are we in such a hurry? What are they about to do?"

"Well sir," the pilot said, "They're about to drop enough explosives on them sharks to wipe out the entire state of Rhode Island."

"What?" Amanda and Kurt chimed in unison.

At that moment, in the distance a massive explosion lit up the skies for miles and thunder deafened their ears. The helicopter lunged forward from the force of the blast. They had to cover their eyes and look away to protect themselves from the blinding light.

The light eventually dimmed enough that everyone could look back, only to see the darkness of night return.

No one said a word. What could they say anyway? They were absolutely speechless. Amanda and Kurt, of course, had mixed feelings. While they were glad to be alive and happy the sharks would not be able to claim any more lives, they were also sad for the oceanographic world of science. They silently gazed out over the waters where a new order of dominance had been destroyed and pondered whether it was really over. Their dream of a new species of shark had now come to an abrupt end. Had the explosion destroyed all of them?

Kurt continued to gaze out the window, his thoughts in turmoil. *Why do we as a civilization never give it a second thought whether we should extinguish life before we have a chance to understand it?*

CHAPTER FORTY-FIVE

The clear, lukewarm fresh water felt good compared to the morning humidity that hung heavily twenty miles inland above the Florida Everglades. The air was thick. They had awoken from their slumber and were now on their daily routine of survival, searching for plant life to supplement their large diet as they migrated slowly southward. Soon cooler weather would set in, and they needed the significantly warmer climate to survive.

The female manatee and her calf of five months had flourished this season, except for the few near misses with boats and their dangerous slicing propellers. The mother had war scars tattooed across her back to show of her past encounters, and she was not about to let that happen to her baby. The calf had grown to well above the normal weight and was as healthy as a sea cow could be.

They gracefully surged forward with mother nodding and prodding her baby downstream, surfacing every so often for oxygen and continuing the journey towards their southern destination. The calf playfully swam ahead of her mother fifteen or so yards away. The mother kept a watchful eye on her, yet she also gave her the freedom to experiment and play, as all calves do. Her full attention and focus was given to her calf, which was certainly her undoing.

The calf turned towards her mother as she heard a bellowing moan. The once placid and transparent waters were now a rich mass of murkiness. Her confusion mounted. She had never experienced this in her life. The waters were darkened by the upheaval of dirt, algae, and blood, making it all but impossible to see the struggle beyond her vision. The wailing shrieks of her mother and the thrashing force within the caliginous waters confused her even more. She floated, motionless, waiting for her mother to emerge from the carnage—believing at anytime the waters would clear and everything would be at peace once again.

The waters finally fell still and she paused to listen for her mother—no sound. Instinct told her she was now alone and that she had became the hunted.

Rising upward for air, she slowly propelled herself in the opposite direction of where she and her mother had traveled before. She felt a threatening presence lurking behind her and frantically swam away as quickly as she could—not fast enough. Her mother was gone and intuitively her mind told her to flee.

Gradually, she crossed over into clearer waters. Her range of vision became full, but behind her still nothing could be seen, but dusky waters. She trudged ahead, tiring herself to exhaustion as she pushed her heavy body up once again for oxygen.

Before she could even reach the surface, a powerful force seized her underside and jerked her downward. Her underbelly was completely sheered off and immense pain overcame her defenseless body. She tried to escape her imminent fate, but it was useless. Her whining squeals for help went unanswered as her attacker's jaws butchered her beyond recognition. She was viciously massacred.

As quickly as the tragedy began, the waters again returned to their natural tranquil state of calmness, and the black terrorizing force dominantly surged northward up the river—to conquer its next victims.

EPILOGUE

Our oceans remain an undiscovered world, barely explored or understood, an abyss of unlearned knowledge that science will never entirely fathom. We have barely scratched the surface, in that respect. One dare not speculate that we as humans have come into contact with, or have discovered, every species or life form that inhabits the vast waters on this planet we call Earth.

What made this previously unknown dominant order of terror, possibly from the bottomless depths of the Atlantic Ocean, leave their habitat? One might speculate any number of hypotheses: A fissure, or opening, in the earth's depths caused by a seaquake or geological shift of the ocean's floor opening a passage from some unrevealed underwater world. Feeding depletion. Atmospheric conditions. Any unexplainable phenomenon.

Does this explain the strange tales and disappearances that have plagued our seas throughout time? This new evil kills for the thrill of the kill, annihilating everything within their path. They have claimed their rightful place at the top of the food chain in our seas, hunting all who dare enter their domain.

Mankind has yet to fully taste their fury. Heaven help us—

*Until the mid-sixteenth century, the fear-provoking monster of the deep we know today as the shark was first known as the Spanish word—**Tiburón**.*

Edward A. Holsclaw II is the author of

Tiburon

Laid to Rest

Origin: Unknown

Twist of Fate

Wisdom from Above

End Days

Claw Marks

Malangus: The Graphic Novel

Mothman Returns

Bigfoot

Origin Unknown: The Graphic Novel - Book One

Mimps: The Graphic Novel

Broken

Unearth - Edward A. Holsclaw II's Ultimate Horror Collection

The Legend of Old Man Crank

He has written many short stories and other literary works. He has won countless writing awards. He writes Horror, Thrillers, Sci-fi/Fantasy, Poetry, and Graphic Novels.